TRAINING

Gymnasium

Englisch 8. Klasse

Lesen • Schreiben • Hören • Wortschatz

Birgit Holtwick
Uta Schein

STARK

Autorinnen:

Birgit Holtwick
unterrichtet seit vielen Jahren Englisch am Gymnasium und arbeitet in der Lehreraus- und fortbildung. Ihre praktische Erfahrung teilt sie auch in ihren Publikationen. Sie veröffentlichte beim Stark Verlag bereits mehrere Bücher und Unterrichtsbeiträge.

Uta Schein
begann ihre langjährige Lehrtätigkeit am Gymnasium als Englisch- und Geschichtslehrerin im bilingualen Zweig. Ihre vielfältigen Erfahrungen aus der Unterrichtspraxis spiegeln sich im Kapitel zum Kompetenzbereich *writing*.

Inhalt

MP3-Tracks

Listening

Words and Spelling

Mediation

Sprecher*innen: Daniel Beaver, Em Filer, Jennifer Mikulla, Roger Voight

Die Hintergrundgeräusche bei den MP3s stammen aus folgenden Quellen: *freesound, pacdv*

Vorwort

Liebe Schülerin, lieber Schüler,

du möchtest dich in Englisch verbessern? Dabei kann dir dieses Buch helfen. Es bietet dir Unterstützung in den verschiedenen Kompetenzbereichen. Du findest jeweils ein Kapitel zum **Lesen**, zum **Hören**, zum **Wortschatz**, zur **Sprachmittlung** und zum **Schreiben**.

Vielleicht weißt du schon aus Klassenarbeiten oder von deiner Englischlehrerin / deinem Englischlehrer, in welchem dieser Bereiche du schwerpunktmäßig arbeiten solltest. Dann kannst du dir gezielt die entsprechenden Kapitel in diesem Buch vornehmen. Ansonsten kannst du auch die Kapitel wählen, die für die nächste Klassenarbeit besonders relevant sind. Bei dem Kapitel „Words and Spelling" kann es auch sinnvoll sein, dass du dir die Topics ansiehst, die für dich gerade inhaltlich aktuell sind.

Hier noch einige Hinweise zum Umgang mit dem Buch:

- Jedes Kapitel beginnt mit einer kurzen **Einführung**, dann folgen mehrere **Texte** und **Übungen**, die nach und nach schwieriger werden.
- In jedem Kapitel werden verschiedene **Tricks und Techniken** vorgestellt, wie du leichter lernen kannst, z. B. wie du dir Wörter besser merkst oder wie du mit bestimmten Aufgabentypen leichter zurechtkommst. Diese Tipps findest du in farbigen Kästen mit dem Titel **„Step up!"**.
- Am Ende jedes Kapitels kannst du in einer Aufgabe die wichtigsten Strategien noch einmal sammeln.
- Alle **Hörverstehenstexte**, die du für Übungen in den Kapiteln *Listening, Words and Spelling* und *Mediation* benötigst, kannst du dir auf der Plattform „MyStark" über deinen persönlichen Zugangscode, den du auf der Umschlaginnenseite findest, herunterladen.
- Ebenso findest du im Buch ein **Vokabelverzeichnis**, das dir die Wörter erklärt, die du nicht kennst oder die du vielleicht wieder vergessen hast.
- Selbstverständlich gibt es zu allen Übungen auch **Lösungen**.

Wir wünschen dir viel Spaß und Erfolg bei der Arbeit mit diesem Buch!

Birgit Holtwick | Uta Schein

Reading –
Wie du deine Lesekompetenz verbessern kannst

Genauso unterschiedlich wie die Texte, die wir lesen, sind auch unsere **Lesestile**. Wenn wir uns einen Überblick über einen Text verschaffen wollen, lesen wir auf eine andere Art und Weise, als wenn wir ganz bestimmte Informationen aus einem Text herausfiltern möchten. Wenn wir einen Text detailliert verstehen wollen, müssen wir zudem interpretieren, was zwischen den Zeilen steht.

- Es ist also sinnvoll, sich **vor dem Lesen** bewusst zu machen, zu welchem Zweck man einen Text liest. Du solltest dich gedanklich vorbereiten, damit es dir dann beim Lesen leichter fällt, den Text zu verstehen. Wie diese Vorarbeit aussehen kann, erfährst du in diesem Kapitel.
- **Während des Lesens** solltest du immer einen Stift zur Hand haben, um wichtige Passagen zu markieren oder am Rand Stichworte zu notieren. So findest du einzelne Textstellen später schneller wieder, wenn du **nach dem Lesen** die Aufgaben bearbeitest.
- Während du das Kapitel zum Leseverstehen durcharbeitest, erhältst du viele Hinweise, die dir das Verstehen und Bearbeiten von fremdsprachlichen Texten erleichtern. Zu diesen sogenannten **Lesestrategien** wirst du auch entsprechende Aufgaben bearbeiten.
- Wir empfehlen dir, das Kapitel in der hier vorliegenden Reihenfolge durchzuarbeiten. Im ersten Topic lernst du, wie du mit **unbekannten Wörtern** umgehst. Diese Strategien kannst du dann in allen anderen Topics anwenden. Im Laufe des Kapitels werden die Texte zudem zunehmend komplexer und der Schwierigkeitsgrad der Aufgaben nimmt zu.
- Am Ende des Kapitels kannst du dir eine **Übersicht** über alle Strategien, die du vor, während oder nach dem Lesen anwenden kannst, erstellen. Du solltest diese Strategien zukünftig immer im Kopf haben, wenn du einen Text liest, damit du sie weiter trainierst und schließlich automatisch anwendest.

Topic 1: Dealing with unknown words

Step up!

Strategien beim Umgang mit unbekannten Wörtern:

1 ***Skip the word***
Du kannst das Wort ignorieren, wenn du den Text auch so verstehst. Diese Technik ist gerade bei längeren Texten oder beim Überfliegen eines Textes sehr wichtig.

2 ***Word family***
Wenn du Wörter aus der gleichen Wortfamilie kennst, kannst du dir die Bedeutung des Wortes davon ableiten, z. B. *anger* → *angry*.

3 ***Other languages***
Vielleicht kennst du ein ähnliches Wort im Deutschen oder in einer anderen Sprache, z. B. *immigration* = Immigration. Aber Vorsicht vor sogenannten *false friends*!

4 ***Context***
Oft kannst du dir die Bedeutung aus dem Zusammenhang erschließen, z. B. *curfew: The teacher imposed a curfew. Pupils were not allowed to leave the hostel between 9 p.m. and 8 a.m.*

5 ***Dictionary***
Du kannst auch ein Wörterbuch zu Rate ziehen; allerdings sollte das nicht allzu häufig sein, da dadurch gerade in Prüfungssituationen viel wertvolle Zeit verlorengehen kann. ■

1 Read the sentences. Use strategies 2–4 from the Step up!-box above to understand the words underlined. Tick the strategy you have used and write down a German translation of the word in the table on the next page. Sometimes you can use more than one strategy.

- Begging certainly isn't fun but some people have to do it out of necessity.
- Both planes were allowed to take off simultaneously.
- Mary was frustrated. Her company had relocated her from Liverpool to London and life was so terribly expensive there.
- My grandmother only wore black clothes when she was in mourning for my grandfather, who had died unexpectedly.
- Karl has never heard a bird sing. He has been totally deaf since birth.
- They opened their hotel three years ago and by now it has turned into a profitable business.

	word family	other languages	context	German translation
out of necessity	☐	☐	☐	
simultaneously	☐	☐	☐	
frustrated	☐	☐	☐	
relocate	☐	☐	☐	
in mourning	☐	☐	☐	
unexpectedly	☐	☐	☐	
deaf	☐	☐	☐	
profitable	☐	☐	☐	

2 False Friends

a) Read the English sentences and the given translation. Decide if the word underlined is a false friend or not. If it is a false friend, correct the translation.

Step up!

False friends

Sogenannte *false friends* sind Wörter, die man gerne verwechselt, weil sie sich z. B. im Deutschen und Englischen zwar ähneln, aber doch etwas Anderes meinen (dt.: „aktuell" heißt auf Englisch beispielsweise nicht *actual* sondern *topical*; *actual* bedeutet „tatsächlich"). ■

False friend? Yes No

- She has hardly worked for the exam. – *Sie hat hart für die Prüfung gearbeitet.* ☑ ☐

  correction: Sie hat kaum für die Prüfung gearbeitet.

- The doctor gave him a receipt. – *Der Arzt gab ihm ein Rezept.* ☐ ☐

  correction: ____________________

- The baker got up early. – *Der Bäcker stand früh auf.* ☐ ☐

  correction: ____________________

- He always spends a lot of money. – *Er spendet immer viel Geld.* ☐ ☐

  correction: ____________________

- The documentary about snakes is interesting. – *Der Dokumentarfilm über Schlangen ist interessant.* ☐ ☐

  correction: ____________________

- She's really brave. – *Sie ist wirklich brav.* ☐ ☐

  correction: ____________________

- He is also a good friend of mine. – *Er ist also ein guter Freund von mir.* ☐ ☐

  correction: ____________________

- She can run fast for 5 kilometres. – *Sie kann fast 5 Kilometer lang rennen.* ☐ ☐

  correction: ____________________

b) Now check if the German sentences are translated correctly. If there is a false friend, improve the translation *(correction)*.

False friend? Yes No

- *Ich möchte dich nicht blamieren.* – I don't want to blame you. ☐ ☐

  correction: ____________________

- *Er stand in der Nähe der Boxen (Musik).* – He was standing close to the boxes. ☐ ☐

  correction: ____________________

- *Ich würde gerne ein Instrument spielen.* – I would like to play an instrument. ☐ ☐

  correction: ____________________

- *In der Schule wird er gemobbt.* – He is mobbed at school. ☐ ☐

  correction: ____________________

- *Das hat er wohl überhört.* – Obviously he has overheard it. ☐ ☐

  correction: ____________________

- *Sei still.* – Be still. ☐ ☐

  correction: ____________________

Topic 2: Signs around the world

Read the different signs and the statements below the signs. Underline keywords in the statements. Then decide if the statements are *true*, *false* or *not given*. Tick (✓) the correct box.

3

Step up!

Aufgabentyp
„true/false/not given"

- Beachte immer genau, was verlangt wird. Markiere dazu in der Aufgabe Schlüsselwörter.
- **Lies** dir die Sätze **genau** durch, da manchmal einzelne Wörter mit dem Ausgangstext übereinstimmen, aber die Aussage trotzdem falsch ist.
- Wenn du eine Aussage am Text **nicht belegen oder widerlegen** kannst, kreuze „not given" an.
- Überlege dir bei „*false*" zur Überprüfung auch, wie der Satz richtigerweise lauten müsste. ■

	true	false	not given
a) Marine stingers can seriously hurt swimmers.	☐	☐	☐
b) During the summer months people are not allowed to swim there.	☐	☐	☐

4

	true	false	not given
a) If you jump from the cliff, you may get badly hurt.	☐	☐	☐
b) If you need to be rescued, you will have to pay $ 150.	☐	☐	☐

5

	true	false	not given
a) The sign is at the top of Africa's highest mountain.	☐	☐	☐
b) Uhuru is an active volcano.	☐	☐	☐

6

	true	false	not given
a) The sign warns travellers not to get close to the "Min Min Light".	☐	☐	☐
b) No one knows where this light comes from.	☐	☐	☐

7

	true	false	not given
a) The signs inform you where you are standing.	☐	☐	☐
b) They have been put up on the Equator.	☐	☐	☐
c) On the opposite side of the earth is Perth, Australia.	☐	☐	☐

8

	true	false	not given
a) Students are not allowed inside this building.	☐	☐	☐
b) Students who stay away from class will have to pay a fine.	☐	☐	☐

9

	true	false	not given
a) The sign addresses people playing golf.	☐	☐	☐
b) It tells people to be careful of cars crossing.	☐	☐	☐

Topic 3: Study and travel

10 Before you start reading, have a look at the text and the pictures on the next page.

a) What kind of text is it?

- ☐ a newspaper article
- ☐ a brochure
- ☐ an advert
- ☐ a catalogue

b) What do you think the aim of the text is?

The aim of the text is to ...

- ☐ explain how students can learn a foreign language best.
- ☐ make the reader book a language course.
- ☐ make children learn their vocabulary in groups rather than alone.
- ☐ give information about different countries and cultures.

c) Which of these words could you expect to read in a text like this?

- ☐ passive
- ☐ active
- ☐ vocabulary
- ☐ party
- ☐ teacher
- ☐ catalogue
- ☐ alone
- ☐ youthful

Step up!

Die Vorbereitung auf den Text

- Stelle vor dem Lesen bereits **Vermutungen** an, worum es in dem Text gehen könnte. Das erleichtert dir das Lesen.
- Überlege dir, was dir **Bilder** oder eine **Überschrift** über den Inhalt verraten können.
- Am Layout erkennst du oft die **Textsorte** (z. B. E-Mail, Zeitungsartikel, Werbeanzeige); wenn du weißt, was für eine Textsorte vorliegt, kannst du dir auch schon in etwa vorstellen, was dich erwartet. Ein Artikel will in der Regel informieren, eine Werbeanzeige zum Kauf eines Produkts anregen usw.
- Ebenso kannst du vorab bereits überlegen, welchen **Wortschatz** du für den Text benötigen wirst. ■

Text Study and travel

1 **You think learning and holidays don't go together? Then you haven't tried our Study and Travel Programme yet!**

2 Our courses are highly effective because here you can study in a relaxed atmosphere and in small groups. Instead of cramming vocabulary on your own, you'll work with a motivated group and friendly teachers. You won't be doing any boring exercises but really be communicating with each other.

What's more, you will keep learning after class, as you'll be in a country where you'll be speaking the language in everyday life.

3 **Why travel with us?**

* Meet young people from all around the world
* Be active and have fun
* Experience new cultures
* Youthful and motivated teachers
* 20 years of experience in the business
* Best value for money

4 **Choose your favourite language and destination:**

English in Brighton or Eastbourne – from £ 350
French in Biarritz or Nice – from £ 340
German in Hamburg – from £ 370
Italian in Florence – from £ 290
Spanish in Granada – from £ 300

5 **For further information** you can ...
call our friendly staff: +44 356 600 1000,
send us an e-mail: info@studyandtravel.com
or download our catalogue here.

11 Answer the following questions, using one to five words or numbers.
First of all read the questions and mark keywords, then scan the text "Study and travel" and write down in which paragraph you can find matching keywords in the text. Then read the passages that you need in more detail.

> **Step up!**
> **„Scannen"**
> - Lies die Aufgabenstellung durch und markiere **Schlüsselwörter**.
> - Überfliege anschließend den Text und **suche gezielt** nach diesen und ähnlichen Wörtern.
> - Lies dann die entsprechenden Textpassagen genauer, um die Aufgaben lösen zu können. ■

a) Say why the programme is so **effective**. Give three reasons.

Paragraph needed: 2 Keyword(s) in the text: effective

- relaxed atmosphere
- ______
- ______

b) Give three reasons for booking a course with "Study and travel".

Paragraph needed: ______ Keyword(s):

- ______
- ______
- ______

c) Name three languages that are taught.

Paragraph needed: ______ Keyword(s):

- ______ • ______ • ______

d) Which destination is the least expensive one and how much does it cost?

Paragraph needed: ______ Keyword(s):

destination: ______ price: ______

e) Name two ways of contacting staff at "Study and travel".

Paragraph needed: ______ Keyword(s):

- ______
- ______

Topic 4: Whale watching

12 Read the conversation between Phil and Tom, then fill in the table below.
Put the paragraphs from the text (A–L) in the correct order (1–12).

Step up!

Aufgabentyp „Putting paragraphs into the correct order"

- Um einen Text in seine ursprüngliche Reihenfolge zu bringen, beginnst du am besten mit dem **Anfang** und dem **Ende**. Diese Bausteine zu erkennen, fällt meist leichter.
- Im Mittelteil solltest du nach **logischen Verbindungen** suchen (z. B. Fragen und dazu passende Antworten).
- Lies den Text am Ende in der **Reihenfolge**, die du festgelegt hast, um zu prüfen, ob alles sinnvoll zusammenpasst. ■

1	2	3	4	5	6	7	8	9	10	11	12
			B							L	

Text **Whale watching**

A PHIL: Oh, I'm afraid you got me wrong there … I wasn't thinking of your safety but of the whales. I guess they must get pretty annoyed or even scared if people come close to them and follow them with their boats.

B PHIL: Whale watching! Isn't that dangerous?

C TOM: Oh, I see what you mean, but I think you've got it wrong. As I said, we didn't get close. We stopped about 200 metres from the whales and just watched them from a distance. And then – you won't believe this – they came closer to us. They really seemed curious to explore our boat and they even dived underneath it. That was really an exciting moment, and probably dangerous too, but it all seemed pretty safe at the time.

D PHIL: I'll see. If ever I happen to travel to the US or Australia, I'll think about it. OK, now I have to run. I have an appointment at the doctor's. See you.

E TOM: Well, it can be. But if you travel with a responsible operator, they make sure that you're safe. You mustn't get too close to the animals because they're so huge, they might destroy the boat with a flip of their tail.

F PHIL: Well, that certainly sounds great and a little scary as well. Still, I'm not so sure. Your presence could affect the whales in ways we don't realise. I mean, the noise of the boat or the people must be terrible for the whales because they have such a fine sense of hearing.

G TOM: Hi Phil, how are you? Long time no see. I've just returned from a trip to Australia.

H PHIL: Wow, that sounds interesting. I've never been to Australia. What did you enjoy most?

I TOM: You've probably got a point there. But our crew told us not to make any loud noises and they really checked that people were behaving in the right way once we were close to the whales. The captain even turned off the motor. Plus, I guess people who have the opportunity to meet whales will never want to hurt them because they will appreciate their beauty much more. They might even help to protect them.

J PHIL: On second thoughts, tours like that might even help to save whales because the people realise that you can earn more money by showing tourists living whales than by hunting and killing them.

K TOM: That's a tough question. But I think the whale watching tour that we did off the east coast was the most exciting part of our trip.

L TOM: Absolutely. So maybe you should try it yourself one day.

Tip Before you go on with the other exercises, check if you have come up with the correct order.

13 Read the whole text (see p. 152) again. While reading, highlight passages in which Phil and Tom argue for and against whale watching. Complete the table to sum up the arguments.

Step up!

Pro und Contra

Bei argumentativen Texten, die das Für und Wider einer Sache behandeln, ist es oft hilfreich, die Argumente im Anschluss an das Lesen in einer Tabelle aufzulisten. ■

Arguments against whale watching	Arguments for whale watching

14 Read the statements and copy one to ten words from the text to show that the statements are correct.
The first one has been done for you.

Step up!

Schlüsselbegriffe
Lies dir zunächst alle Aussagen durch und markiere Wörter, die dir besonders wichtig erscheinen. Suche dann für jeden **Schlüsselbegriff** im Dialog Sätze mit Wörtern des gleichen **Wortfeldes** oder **Synonyme** (= Wörter mit gleicher Bedeutung). ■

Statements	Words from the text
It's difficult for Tom to decide what he liked best about his trip to Australia.	*That's a tough question.*
Whales can damage ships easily.	
Tom misunderstood Phil.	
Tom felt secure on the ship.	
Whales can hear very well.	
Phil is considering doing whale watching himself one day.	
Phil is in a hurry.	

15 What have you learned about the right behaviour on whale watching tours? Write down three rules that people need to follow before and during a tour.

- ______________________________
- ______________________________
- ______________________________

Topic 5: Summer camp

16 What do you think the text will be about? Look at the pictures and consider what kind of text it is. Then write your ideas down in note form.

Text Summer camp – Michael's Blog

Day 1

Today I arrived at the summer camp in British Columbia, Canada. I was very excited because it was the first time that I had been on a plane trip on my own. When I arrived in Vancouver, a guy from the camp picked me and some other teenagers up and took us to the camp.
When I saw my room, I was pretty annoyed because I have to share the room with three other boys. Man, that's tough because it means that I won't have any **privacy** for the next two weeks.

Day 3

The other boys in my room are quite OK. Sometimes it's a bit hard to communicate because they come from Mexico, Brazil and Italy. But, hey, I'm the lucky one really because José, Miguel and Antonio have got English lessons five days a week, three hours a day. **What a drag**! And I thought this was a holiday camp! Well, it is for me. I'm outdoors most of the day and go swimming or play soccer and yesterday I also tried golf. It's harder than it looks, really. The food here is nice and the other guys are mostly pretty cool. I spend a lot of time with Carl. He's from Florida and we've become mates, kind of.

Day 5

I'm getting bored. Mum and I agreed that I could do the "Adventure Tour" and they promised kayaking and rock climbing, but so far we've only been preparing for the big trip. The trainers keep telling us we need to get ready "for the real thing". So I have to learn **survival skills**, like what to do if we see a bear, which wild berries to eat, how to make a fire and so on. I'll take my **lighter** anyway, just in case. We also learn about first aid and do a lot of planning, like what gear to select, what clothes and shoes to pack and what food to take along.

Day 6

Another day of planning our trip but, hey, now we're done. Tomorrow we'll be off into the **wilderness**. I'm really looking forward to this. My backpack is pretty heavy so I hope we won't have to walk for too many miles. Tonight I'll try to get some more sleep because we're leaving pretty early. Carl will come, too.

Day 13

Man, that was great. It was really worth all the preparation. We spent five days in the wilderness and went rock climbing, kayaking and mountain biking. We returned yesterday but I was so **exhausted** that I had to rest for a day before I felt like doing anything at all. It was incredible, the scenery was just brilliant and the rock climbing was extremely cool. But now **I'm aching** all over … Phew, I'll have to rest some more and then I need to pack my bag because tomorrow I'll be on my way home again. What a pity.

17 Look at the words/phrases from the text. Read the sentences they appear in again. Use the strategies to deal with unknown words (see p. 2) to try to understand them. Then match the expressions with their correct German translations by filling in the correct letters. The first one (F) has been done for you. There are four more German meanings than you need.

Expression	Letter
privacy	☐
survival skills	☐
What a drag!	F
wilderness	☐
lighter	☐
ache	☐
exhausted	☐

A) Wildnis
B) erschöpft
C) Privatsphäre
D) Überlebenstechniken
E) Übertreibung
F) Wie langweilig
G) leichtgläubig
H) weh tun
I) Überlebenstraining
J) Wüste
K) Feuerzeug
L) Was für ein Glück

18 Mark passages in the text that tell you how Michael feels at the summer camp.

19 Answer the following questions about Michael's feelings in one or two sentences each.

Step up!

Stimmungen und Emotionen von Personen
Eine Person kann deutlich sagen, wie sie sich fühlt. Oft wird sie ihre **Gefühle** aber nur indirekt zum Ausdruck bringen. Dann musst du zwischen den Zeilen lesen, d. h., du musst **interpretieren**, was mit den Wörtern ausgesagt werden soll. ■

a) How does Michael feel on his first day at the summer camp? Why?

He is excited because everything is new to him. When he sees his room, he is annoyed because …

b) Why does he get bored after a few days?

c) What are his feelings after the survival trip to the wilderness? Why?

d) How does he feel about the end of his stay at the summer camp? Why?

Topic 6: Amit, an undocumented immigrant

20 At school you are doing a project about young illegal immigrants in the USA. Skim the text and decide if the text would be interesting for your school project. Briefly explain why you think so.

Step up!

„Skimmen“

Bevor du einen Text genau liest, solltest du ihn zunächst nur grob **überfliegen**:

- Du kannst z. B. nur **Überschriften** und Zwischenüberschriften lesen sowie ggf. Grafiken und Bilder betrachten.
- Du kannst auch nur den ersten und den letzten **Absatz** lesen oder von jedem Absatz nur den ersten Satz.

„*Skimming*“ ist besonders hilfreich, wenn du viel Material hast und erst grob **filtern** willst, was für dich von Bedeutung ist, z. B. wenn du etwas im Internet recherchierst. ■

Text **Amit, an undocumented immigrant**

1 I was ten years old when I left my mom and my dad in Sri Lanka. I didn't really know what was happening when my mom took me to Colombo International Airport. There we met a woman I had never seen before. My mom said she was my aunt, though. Then I took my small suitcase, which my mom had bought for me, and boarded a plane for the first time in my life.

2 My aunt took me to my grandparents in California. I had never seen them before either, but I knew that my grandpa often sent money to support my family because my father couldn't work any longer after a bad accident. I guess I would never have left my parents if they hadn't promised to follow me soon, but it turned out that this was a lie. I guess I figured this out when I found a photo showing my parents and myself in my suitcase. But I'm not mad at my parents; I know that it was hard for them to send me thousands of miles away. They simply hoped that I would have a better life here in the United States.

3 I promised myself that I would not disappoint them and so I worked hard at school. I enjoyed learning the new language and also other languages and I also liked Math. I made some friends and my teachers were mostly nice. I even managed to win a spelling and a reading competition. My parents and my grandparents were proud of me and over the years, everything seemed to be normal.

4 But one day I realized that I was different from my friends. However, it was not my outward appearance or my family situation. Many of my classmates didn't live with both of their parents and our school was very multicultural. No, it was something else.

5 One day I wanted to register to get my driver's permit. Most of my friends already had theirs, so I thought it was time for me to get one, too. The clerk at the office needed an official document to prove that I was a permanent resident, so I showed her my Green Card. She looked at it closely, handed it back to me and whispered: "It is fake, don't show it to anyone and don't come back here." I was utterly confused. What did she mean, it was fake?

6 Quickly, I returned home to my grandpa and asked him about my Green Card. My grandpa looked at me and I could see that he was deeply sad. Yes, he said, he had bought false papers for me, so I could stay with them. That's when I realized that I was an illegal immigrant in a country that I had long learned to see as my home.

21 Which summary fits the text best?

A young immigrant from Sri Lanka …

- [ ] is found to be an illegal resident in the USA.
- [ ] tells of his experience as an undocumented immigrant in the USA.
- [ ] moves to the USA with his family and grows up there.
- [ ] tries to get hold of a fake Green Card to be able to get his driver's license.

22 Match the headlines (A–H) with the different paragraphs in the text (1–6). There are two headlines more than you need.

A Success at school
B False papers
C My driver's license
D Leaving home
E Grandpa's secret
F A new start
G False promise
H Being different

paragraph	1	2	3	4	5	6
headline						

23 Answer the questions by ticking (✓) the right answer.

a) Why did Amit have to leave his home?
- ☐ His grandparents wanted him to come and live with them.
- ☐ His parents hoped he would have a better life in the USA.
- ☐ His uncle took him with him to the USA.
- ☐ His father had died in an accident.

Step up!

Aufgabentyp „*Multiple Choice*"
- Meist wird nur **eine richtige Lösung** gesucht; vergewissere dich trotzdem stets, ob das auch der Fall ist.
- Lies immer alle Auswahlmöglichkeiten genau durch und suche die entsprechende(n) **Textstelle(n)**, auf die sich die Aussagen beziehen.
- Manchmal lassen sich Antworten auch durch das **Ausschlussverfahren** finden, das heißt, du musst überlegen, welche Antworten auf keinen Fall stimmen können. ■

b) How did Amit's grandpa support the family?
- ☐ He registered Amit with the local police in the USA.
- ☐ He got Amit's father a job after his accident.
- ☐ He paid for Amit's ticket to the USA.
- ☐ He sent them money to Sri Lanka.

c) How does Amit learn that he is an undocumented immigrant?
- ☐ His classmates show him their driver's license.
- ☐ A clerk tells him that his driver's license is fake.
- ☐ His grandpa tells him that his papers are false.
- ☐ Amit finds out that his Green Card has expired.

Topic 7: Studying abroad

24 Skim the text.

a) Find out what kind of text it is and what it might be about.

____

____

____

____

____

b) Who do you think the text might interest?

- ☐ Young people who want to study in China
- ☐ Math teachers in China
- ☐ Young people who want to study in Australia
- ☐ English teachers in the USA

Text

Studying abroad

International students enrich our society
by Susan Parker, Sydney

There are different ways in which international students contribute to our society. They make our communities more diverse and enrich them with their own cultures. What is more, they make Australia's global networks stronger. These students only come here for a limited period of time and then return to their home countries or move on to another country. However, the connection they have formed with our country will often last a lifetime. In times of globalisation, these connections are very important and extremely valuable.

Of course, international students also profit from their stay in Australia. Most importantly, they get a high quality education, which is internationally accepted. But it is also a unique experience, which helps to form one's personality.

In order to become an international student, people must take different steps, such as enrolling in a course they are interested in. Only if they are accepted for full-time study can they get a student visa. They must also have a certain amount of money, be in good health and meet certain conditions concerning their character.

Most international students come from China. In 2014 almost 34 % were of Chinese origin, followed by India and Malaysia, with Malaysian students accounting for only about 5 % of the international students.

In the years 2011 - 2012 the number of Indian students had fallen considerably, with only 5 - 6 % of the international students coming from India. In 2014 their number was back up again and they accounted for almost 10 % of the international students. The temporary decline was partly because of cases of violence against international students. Indian students in particular no longer felt safe here. However, 90 % of all international students are still happy with their study situation and living conditions as well as with their safety while studying.

Most international students come to Australia for higher education. Therefore, the majority (48 %) are 20 - 24 years old, about one third (28 %) are 25 – 29 years old and only 10 % are 15 - 19 years old.

There is a pretty equal share of male and female students, but that number varies a lot depending on the country of origin. For instance, 63 % of the students from India and Nepal are men, whereas 62 % of the students from Thailand and the USA are women.

Even though studying abroad has a lot of advantages for the individual students, for the communities they move to and for those they come from, only 10.5 % of all Australian students study abroad. Most of those study in an English-speaking country. Thus, 28 % of all Australian students studying abroad stay close to home and only move to New Zealand. 30 % study in the USA, followed by the UK (15 %) and Canada (5 %). Only 3 % choose German universities. As a consequence we need to encourage more of our students to leave their home country in order to improve their cultural understanding and create international networks.

Step up!

Möglichkeiten, einen Text besser zu verstehen

- Bei längeren Texten ist es hilfreich, ihn in **Sinnabschnitte** (= *sense units*) zu unterteilen. Ein **Stichwort** oder eine **Überschrift** zu jedem Sinnabschnitt hilft dir später, dich schneller im Text zu orientieren.
- Du kannst dir auch Oberbegriffe, zu denen man Informationen im Text findet, überlegen. Lege dann eine **Tabelle** an und sammle alle wichtigen Informationen.
- Eine weitere Möglichkeit ist eine **Mindmap**, die die wichtigsten Informationen aus dem Text und ihren Zusammenhang darstellt. ■

25 Subdivide the article into sense units and find a headline for each unit.

lines	headline
ll. 1–7	Advantages for Australia

26 Complete the tables.

a)

percentage	countrys of origin in 2014
	China
	India
5 %	

b)

male	female	country of origin
54 %	46 %	overall
	-	Nepal
-		USA

27 You want to tell somebody else what you have found out from the text. Make a mind map to structure your notes.

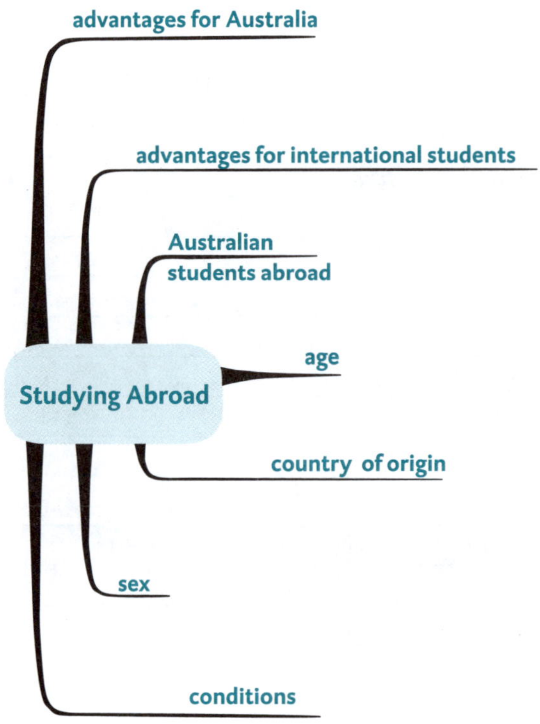

Topic 8: Chat rooms

28 First you should get an overview of the text to find out what it is about. To do so, choose a style of reading (a) and a strategy (b). Then take some notes to complete the table below (c).

Step up!

Lesestil und -strategien
Lies die jeweilige Aufgabe zum Text gut durch und mache dir klar, was genau gefordert ist. Wähle dann geeignete **Lesestile** (= *styles of reading*) und **Strategien** (= *strategies*) aus. ■

a) Choose a **style of reading**.

- ☐ "Scan" the text (see Topic 3).
- ☐ "Skim" the text (see Topic 6).

b) Choose suitable **strategies**.

- ☐ Take notes while reading.
- ☐ Underline keywords.
- ☐ Look up all unknown words.
- ☐ Subdivide into sense units.

c) Complete the table with information from the text.

Step up!

Die wesentlichen Informationen eines Textes kannst du erfassen, indem du die W-Fragen beantwortest. Dies gelingt zum Beispiel in einer Tabelle sehr übersichtlich. ■

Who?	
Where?	
When?	
What?	
Why?	

Text My mum says that when she was young she had penfriends, people she used to write letters to in different countries. Friends on the Internet is not much different from that, really. The thing is that instead of writing with a pen, going down to the post office, putting the envelope in a red box and waiting weeks for a reply, it's instant. My mum is also dead nosy. She has a habit of standing over me when I'm on my computer, cruising from one site to another, and saying, 'What does that mean?' 'Why is it saying that?' and 'What do all those little dots and brackets mean?' And in spite of having all those penfriends when she was younger, she's always been highly suspicious about anything to do with the Internet.

'I've read about girls who use chat rooms,' she said, coming into my room one day soon after I'd started getting to know Zed. 'It was in the paper the other day. A thirteen-year-old girl thought she was writing to a boy the same age, and they got to know each other and met up, and he turned out to be a forty-year-old pervert.'

'I know all that!' I said. 'There's always those scare stories in the papers. I'm not that stupid, though.' And I showed her the stuff that the website made you read before they'd allow you into a chat room – about being sensible and not writing anything rude and never meeting up with someone you didn't know without telling people exactly where you were going.

'And not everyone's a pervert, Mum. One of the teachers at school met another teacher online, and now they're getting married.'

Mum shrugged.

'Anyway, to get into a teenage chat room you have to give your date of birth.'

'Well, that doesn't mean a thing!'

'And people get pulled out of chat rooms if they start talking dirty,' I said. 'There's a sort of supervisor in charge.'

'How does that work, then? You mean there's someone in every single one of those chat rooms monitoring everything that's said?'

'Yeah, I think so,' I said uncertainly.

'Well, even if there is, they can't vet everyone that's speaking. I mean, you could be anyone. You can pretend you're any age you like, or that you're rolling in money, or you're a film star or something. No one's going to come round and check up on you, are they?'

'No, all right!' I said, getting irritated. 'Anyway, I have met someone and he's really nice.'

'You've *met* someone!' she gasped.

'Not actually met. Not in person,' I said. 'I mean, I've met him online.'

'Oh! You gave me a turn there!' she said, fanning herself.

'Look, he's OK. His name's Zed and he –'

'That's never his real name!'

'No. It's his web name. You always have a web name. Mine's Buzybee.'

'Well, how odd. And how old is this boy?'

'Eighteen.'

'Too old for you. That's if he is eighteen. He's probably fifty.'

I groaned.

'If you're going to keep saying things like that I'm not going to tell you about him.'

'OK, I won't say anything else. Go on, then, tell me about him.'

'He's eighteen and he's some sort of sales manager in an office.'

'Manager! At eighteen? I shouldn't think so.'

'Mum!' I said warningly.

I didn't want to tell her at all, really, but I wanted to tell *someone* and she was the only person I had. I told her all the things Zed and I had talked about and how we'd really seemed to hit it off. Funnily enough, when I finished telling her all that stuff she then switched into a different worry mode. From being a mum worried about her daughter meeting a pervert, she became a mum worried about her daughter not having any friends.

'Amy, I'm sure this boy is perfectly nice, but you're not going to spend the rest of your life in this bedroom talking to him, are you?' she said. 'It's a lovely evening and it's light until nine-thirty now. A bit of fresh air would do you good.'

'What? You want me to go round the swings?' I said.

'Don't be silly! I'm just saying that you're always stuck upstairs these days. I thought it was supposed to be boys who were always playing games on their computers.'

'I haven't been playing games! I've been talking to a friend. And anyway, I've finished online for the moment. I'm going to do some school work,' I said. I wasn't, but I wanted her to go so I could have a quiet think about Zed.

From: Hooper, Mary. Amy. Bloomsbury Children's Books. London. 2002

29 Read the text again and highlight information about the <u>characters</u>.

What do you learn about ...

Amy:	
Amy's mother:	
Zed:	

30 Read the statements and compare them to the text. Say if they are *true* or *false*. If a statement is *true*, give the lines where you can find the information in the text.

	Statements	True	False	Lines in the text
a)	Friends on the Internet answer quickly.	☐	☐	
b)	Amy's mum often looks over her daughter's shoulder to see what she is doing online.	☐	☐	
c)	Amy thinks that newspaper articles about chat rooms are made to frighten people.	☐	☐	
d)	Amy always enters her date of birth when she is online.	☐	☐	
e)	There is someone to ensure that the rules on a chat room are followed.	☐	☐	
f)	Amy's mother manages to make her daughter start to doubt chat room safety.	☐	☐	
g)	Amy's mother thinks there are too many people in a chat room to be controlled.	☐	☐	
h)	Zed, Amy's friend, works in a shop.	☐	☐	
i)	Amy's mother is happy that Amy has found a new friend.	☐	☐	
j)	Amy's mother wants her daughter to go outside.	☐	☐	

Topic 9: Life is an open door

31 Read the title and look at the picture. Come up with some ideas about why life might be seen as an open door or as a closed door.

Text

LIFE IS AN OPEN DOOR

Life is an open door,
Open to our talents or closed forever;
Life is a highway running,
Or exited prematurely, at will or by chance;
Life is seldom flat as a plain
Or straight as a chiseled arrow;
Life turns and dips with time and distance;
Nevertheless, life is an open door,
Open to a future untold, but to a future that
We can mold.

From: Poems for Young People, Inspirational, Educational and Therapeutic Poetry by Frederick D. Harper, PhD.

Step up!

Textsorte Gedicht

- Nähere dich einem Gedicht **schrittweise** und lies es mehrfach. Bei jedem Lesen wird dir etwas Neues auffallen.
- Versuche allen Wörtern einen **Sinn** zu geben, sodass am Ende das Gedicht als Ganzes für dich eine **Bedeutung** erhält. Diese Bedeutung kann für verschiedene Leser übrigens durchaus **unterschiedlich** ausfallen. ■

32 a) Read the poem and match the following words with their German meaning.

A prematurely (l. 4) — **1** *Ebene*
B at will (l. 4) — **2** *verfrüht*
C by chance (l. 4) — **3** *gemeißelter Pfeil*
D seldom (l. 5) — **4** *nach Belieben*
E plain (l. 5) — **5** *formen*
F chiseled arrow (l. 6) — **6** *durch Zufall*
G dip (l. 7) — **7** *selten*
H mold (l. 10) — **8** *sich senken*

A	B	C	D	E	F	G	H

b) Explain in a few words what the poem is about.

Step up!

Gedichte arbeiten oft mit sprachlich ausgedrückten Bildern. Daher ist es hilfreich, genau zu schauen, welche Bilder verwendet werden, und zu überlegen, was diese im Textzusammenhang (Kontext) bedeuten könnten. ■

33 Read the poem again. Make sure you understand every single word because in a poem every word is important. Subdivide the poem into sense units and write down the image(s) used.

sense unit (lines)	image

34 Explain what the different images tell you about life.

image (lines)	what it tells you about life

Topic 10: Strategien zum Leseverstehen

35 In diesem Kapitel hast du verschiedene Strategien verwendet, um Lesetexte besser zu verstehen oder Aufgaben leichter lösen zu können. Suche die Lesestrategien in den *Step up!*–Kästen des Kapitels und trage sie in die folgende Tabelle ein. Du musst entscheiden, ob es sich um eine Strategie zum *pre-*, *while-* oder *post-reading* handelt oder ob sie dir hilft, unbekannte Wörter zu erschließen.

Reading-Strategies
Vor dem Lesen: ➡ Vermutungen über den Text anstellen (z. B. S. 9) ➡ ➡ ➡ ➡
Während des Lesens: ➡ Scannen/Schlüsselbegriffe markieren (S. 11) ➡ ➡ ➡ ➡
Wenn ich Wörter nicht verstehe: ➡ ➡ ➡ ➡ ➡
Nach dem Lesen: ➡ Textzusammenfassung ➡ Informationen in Tabelle ergänzen (S. 14) ➡ ➡

Listening –
Wie du gesprochene Texte besser verstehen kannst

Wie bei Lesetexten gibt es auch bei Hörtexten ganz verschiedene Gründe, einen Text zu hören. Daher solltest du dir **vor dem Hören** bewusst machen, mit welchem Ziel du einen Text hörst, damit du einen entsprechenden **Hörstil** verwenden kannst.

- Wir unterscheiden zwischen dem **Globalverständnis**, bei dem du verstehen möchtest, worum es in dem Text geht,
- und dem **Detailverständnis**, bei dem du möglichst viele Einzelheiten mitbekommen möchtest.
- Im Unterricht solltest du **während des Hörens** immer Papier und Stift bereithalten, um dir Notizen machen zu können, denn dein Gedächtnis kann sich so viele Informationen meist gar nicht auf einmal merken.
- Ziel dieses Kapitels ist es, dir möglichst viele **Strategien** an die Hand zu geben, damit dir das Hörverstehen englischer Texte zunehmend leichter fällt.
- Bei den Aufgaben ist jeweils angegeben, wie oft du einen Text hören sollst. Denke stets daran, dass du gesprochene Texte im wirklichen Leben in der Regel nur ein einziges Mal hören kannst. Ziel muss es also sein, das Wichtigste schon beim ersten Hören zu verstehen.
- Am Ende des Kapitels kannst du dir eine Übersicht über alle Strategien, die du vor, während oder nach dem Hören anwenden kannst, erstellen. Lese dir die Strategien, wenn du in Zukunft eine Hörverstehensaufgabe machst, vor dem Hören noch einmal kurz durch, damit du sie weiter trainierst und schließlich automatisch anwendest.
- Im Lösungsteil sind die **Texte** abgedruckt, sodass du sie bei Bedarf oder Interesse lesen kannst.

Topic 11: Plans for the weekend

It is Friday afternoon and you are listening to the radio because you are planning your weekend activities. You would like to know what the weather will be like and what events are on in your area.

Step up!

Vor dem Hören

Bevor du einen Text hörst, solltest du dich darauf einstellen, was dich erwartet; dabei helfen dir die **Überschrift** und die **Aufgaben**. Auch **Bilder** zur Aufgabe können hilfreich sein.
Folgende Fragen lassen sich vor jedem Hörtext anwenden. Nutze diese ***pre-listening activities*** generell beim Hörverstehen:

- Welche **Textsorte** liegt vor?
- Um was geht es im Text?
- Welches Vorwissen zum Thema kann dir nützlich sein?
- Welche Wörter, die mit dem Thema zu tun haben, kennst du schon?
- Musst du für die Beantwortung der Fragen den gesamten Text verstanden haben oder benötigst du nur einzelne Wörter oder Absätze? ■

36 **Weather Forecast**

Before you listen to the text, look at the table in the next exercise and read the following questions. Choose the correct answers.
Be careful: there is usually more than one correct answer.

- From the title and the introduction, what kind of text do you expect?
  - ☐ a podcast
  - ☐ a radio programme
  - ☐ a report
  - ☐ a commercial ad
- What will the text be about?
  - ☐ the weather in the near future
  - ☐ information on past events
  - ☐ stories about celebrities
  - ☐ suggestions on what to do and what to wear in the next few days
- What do you know about the topic?
  - ☐ a forecast is a prediction of the future
  - ☐ in a weather report they often talk about the past
  - ☐ in the UK it rains all the time
  - ☐ in the US temperatures are given in Fahrenheit – not Celsius

- Which words do you already know to be able to talk about the topic? Look at the following pictures and write down verbs, nouns and adjectives.

- Do you need to understand everything or just single words to do the next exercise?

☐ you have to understand the whole text

☐ you have to listen for details and understand single words or numbers

37 a) Before you go on, check your answers to the previous exercise. Then listen to the text once. While listening, complete the table.

Track 01

	Friday	**Saturday**	**Sunday**
highest temperature (°F)			
lowest temperature (°F)			
weather			
suggested activities			

Track 01

b) Look at your answers. Mark those boxes which you could not fill in or where you are not quite sure if your answer is correct. Then listen to the text a second time and focus on those pieces of information.

Step up!

Nach dem (ersten) Hören

Markiere dir nach dem ersten Hördurchgang die Fragen und Aufgabenbereiche, die du noch nicht lösen konntest. Beim **zweiten Hören** kannst du dann besonders auf diese achten. Auch Lösungen, bei denen du dir **unsicher** bist, solltest du markieren, um sie beim nächsten Hören zu **überprüfen.** ■

38 Time for commercials

a) Before you listen to the text, take a minute or two to answer the questions.

- From the title, what kind of texts do you expect?

  ____

- What will the texts be about?

  ____

- What do you know about the topic?

  ____

  ____

- Which words do you know to be able to talk about the topic?

  ____

  ____

- Do you need to understand everything or single words to do task b)?

  ____

Track 02

b) Listen to the text once. What is being advertised?

- First ad: ______________________________
- Second ad: ______________________________
- Third ad: ______________________________

39 Events at Little Rock

a) Before you listen to the text, take a minute or two to answer the questions.

- From the title, what kind of texts do you expect?

  ____

- What will the texts be about?

  ____

- What do you know about the topic?

___

___

___

- Which words do you know to be able to talk about the topic?

___

___

___

- Do you need to understand everything or single words to do task b)?

___

Track 03

b) Listen to the text once. While listening complete the table.

	Event 1	Event 2	Event 3
Who?			
What?			
What day?			
Where?	*Robinson Center in the "Exhibit … "*	*Verizon …*	*Robinson Center in the " "*
What time?			
Ticket price?			

Track 03

c) Look at your answers. Mark those boxes which you could not fill in or where you are not quite sure if you got the answer correct. Then listen to the text a second time and focus especially on those pieces of information.

Topic 12: Planking, owling and milking – The latest web craze

40 a) Look at the pictures and try to match them with the words. There are more words than you need.

A	B	C	D

Annotation
* owl: *Eule*

Track 04

b) Now listen to the first part of the report and answer the questions to get a general idea of what the text is about.

Step up!

Notizen anfertigen

Du kannst dir z. B. **W-Fragen** auf einen Zettel schreiben und diese während des Hörens stichwortartig beantworten. Das ist besonders hilfreich, wenn du den **Text global verstehen** willst, um ihn kurz zusammenzufassen. ■

Who?		
Where?		
When?	1997	2007
What?		
Why?		

41 a) Read the questions in task b). Underline the keywords and find synonyms for them.

Example: What is the position in the "lying down game" compared to?

position = location, place

lying down game = something where people lie completely flat on their front for fun

Step up!

Bevor du Fragen zum Hörtext beantwortest

- Lese dir die Fragen vor dem Hören genau durch und unterstreiche **Schlüsselwörter**.
- Du kannst dir auch **Synonyme** (= andere Wörter mit der gleichen Bedeutung) oder **Umschreibungen** zu den Schlüsselwörtern der Fragen überlegen, denn häufig werden in den Aufgabenstellungen nicht dieselben Wörter wie im Hörtext verwendet. ■

Track 05

b) Listen to the report. Then answer the questions below in 1–5 words. You do not have to write in complete sentences. The first one has already been done for you.

- What is the position in the "lying down game" compared to?

  standing to (or at) attention

- How long did the game take to spread?

___

- How did the game become internationally known?

___

- What is it called in Australia?

___

- What is it called in Ireland?

___

- How did the photos published on Facebook change over time?

___

- Where did the airport worker perform his act?

___

- What does the speaker think of these acts?

___

- Which is the latest web craze?

___

Topic 13: National Aboriginal Day

42 Read the title of the topic and the words in the table below. Also look at the pictures on the next page. Then form two sentences to say what the text will probably be about.

____

____

____

____

____

43 Track 06

Here, nouns and names from the text are given in the list below. While listening to the text, pay special attention to these words and add further information (e. g. verbs, adjectives, adverbs) to the nouns. The more notes you take, the better you will do in the following task. You may listen to the text twice.

Step up!

Wörter notieren

Eine weitere Möglichkeit, **Notizen** während des Hörens anzufertigen, besteht darin, sich auf **einzelne Wörter** zu konzentrieren. Dies sind in der Regel vor allem **Substantive**, **Verben**, **Namen** und **Zahlen**. Versuche, dir beim ersten Hören Wörter zu notieren.
Wenn du beim Anfertigen der Notizen Platz zwischen den einzelnen Wörtern lässt, kannst du bei einem zweiten Hören Ergänzungen vornehmen. Auf diese Weise lässt sich der Text nach dem Hören rekonstruieren. ■

nouns, names	further information
Celebrate Canada	
National Aboriginal Day	
Canada Day	
summer solstice	
Thunder Bay	

44 Read the statements below. Then decide if they are *true*, *false* or *not given* in the text. Try to do the exercise with the help of your notes only. If necessary, listen to the text again.

	true	false	not given
a) Canadians will celebrate their country for 11 days.	☐	☐	☐
b) Events are organised throughout the whole country.	☐	☐	☐
c) National Aboriginal Day is the first event to be celebrated.	☐	☐	☐
d) It will be followed by Canada Day the next day.	☐	☐	☐
e) There are about 1,500,000 Inuit people in Canada.	☐	☐	☐
f) Guests get actively involved in the activities.	☐	☐	☐
g) In dance workshops people can learn traditional dances.	☐	☐	☐
h) The summer solstice marks the day with the fewest hours of light.	☐	☐	☐
i) In Thunder Bay people are invited to watch the rising of the sun together on June 21st.	☐	☐	☐
j) June 21st has been known as National Aboriginal Day since 1969.	☐	☐	☐
k) Aboriginals had to fight for a long time to get their own National Day.	☐	☐	☐

Topic 14: Grade retention

45 a) Have a look at the title first. Then listen to the first part of the text and give a short definition for the phrase "grade retention" without looking it up in a dictionary or on the internet.

Track 07

Step up!

Wörter aus dem Kontext erschließen

Der **Textzusammenhang** kann dir helfen, einzelne Wörter, die du nicht kennst, zu verstehen, z. B.: *He stopped the car, turned off the engine and got out.* → engine muss also der „Motor" sein.

Es gibt Wörter, die oft zusammen auftauchen. Wenn du also das eine verstehst, kannst du das andere Wort erraten, z. B. *summer and winter, last but not least, swimming pool.* Diese nennen wir **Kollokationen.** ■

b) Listen to another part of the text. Some words are missing. Try to find the missing words. Guess from the context and collocations.

Track 08

1 ____________________

2 ____________________

3 ____________________

4 ____________________

5 ____________________

6 ____________________

7 ____________________

46 Now listen to the whole text and tick (✓) the correct answers below.

Track 09

a) Experts say that grade retention costs …

- ☐ up to $ 1.2 million a year.
- ☐ up to $ 1.2 billion a year.
- ☐ at least $ 1.2 million a year.
- ☐ at least $ 1.2 billion a year.

b) Who argues for grade retention?

- ☐ most students
- ☐ most school psychologists
- ☐ Roger, the radio reporter
- ☐ some teachers

c) School psychologists make a connection between grade retention and …
- [ ] where students and their parents come from.
- [ ] gender (girl or boy).
- [ ] success in later life.
- [ ] a feeling of incompetence.

d) The first caller thinks grade retention is helpful because …
- [ ] grade 8 is a difficult year.
- [ ] parents are afraid their children have to repeat a class.
- [ ] it makes students work harder.
- [ ] students are put under pressure by their friends.

e) The second caller thinks grade retention …
- [ ] doesn't help with the real problems.
- [ ] doesn't even help for a short time.
- [ ] happens too often.
- [ ] happens to everybody.

f) The teacher who calls would like to use the money spent on grade retention to …
- [ ] offer students better prospects for the future.
- [ ] pay teachers more money.
- [ ] spend more time with the students.
- [ ] pay for smaller classes.

g) In the end Roger talks to …
- [ ] a secondary school teacher.
- [ ] a student who has to repeat a class.
- [ ] a school psychologist.
- [ ] a parent whose child is in danger of failing.

h) According to Emily Button it is most important that …
- [ ] specialists try to find out more about the issue.
- [ ] parents know more about what their kids do at school.
- [ ] schools support students better.
- [ ] students know about their strengths and weaknesses.

47 Listen to the text once more and write down two arguments for grade retention and five arguments against it. You may stop the recording while you write down the arguments.

Track 09

Arguments for grade retention:

Arguments against grade retention:

Topic 15: A complaint

48 Collect at least three more signal words that you know for each of the five categories. At least one example is given for each category to get you started.

Step up!
Achte beim Hören auf **Signalwörter**. Diese geben dir einen Hinweis darauf, was als Nächstes kommen wird:
- „but" leitet eine Einschränkung oder einen Widerspruch ein: "I liked the place but it was a bit small."
- „and" wird oft in Aufzählungen verwendet, z. B.: "I bought some cheese and ham." ■

a) **Listing** *(Aufzählung)*:

first of all, to begin with, ...

b) **Addition** *(Ergänzung)*:

and, ...

c) **Contrast** *(Gegensatz)*:

but, ...

d) **Reason** *(Begründung)*:

because, ...

e) **Conclusion** *(Schlussfolgerung)*:

all in all, ...

49 Read the title of the topic and the ad below. Form two sentences to say what the text might be about.

Ideally located, close to both Cagliari International Airport and the town centre, this family-run hotel offers the perfect setting for relaxing holidays. The sandy beach that belongs exclusively to the hotel is just 200 m away.

The hotel has been renovated and upgraded. It now features 4 **** facilities and services

Benvenuto in Sardegna

** Ideally located *** Ideally located *** Ideally located *** Ideally located **

50 Listen to the phone call and fill in the form.

Track 10

Sunshine Travels

Client's name: ____________________

Address: ____________________

Telephone: ____________________

E-Mail: ____________________

Booking number: ____________________

Place of residence: ____________________

Complaints: ____________________

____

____

____

____

Client's demand: ____________________

____

Measures suggested: ____________________

____

____

51 Listen to the text. How do the client and the assistant speak on the phone? Choose two adjectives from the lists on the next page to describe their tone of voice at the beginning and towards the end of the conversation. Which information do we get at the beginning and which at the end? How does the information match the feelings expressed? You may use German in this task.

Track 10

Step up!

Manchmal musst du beim Hören interpretieren, also Schlussfolgerungen aus dem, was du gehört hast, ziehen. Bei Hörtexten kann es beispielsweise auch wichtig sein, **wie** die Sprecher reden. Dies gibt dir Aufschluss über deren Gefühle. ■

- The client's tone of voice at the beginning:
  - ☐ polite
  - ☐ joking
  - ☐ friendly
  - ☐ angry
- The assistant's tone of voice at the beginning:
  - ☐ understanding
  - ☐ polite
  - ☐ annoyed
  - ☐ unfriendly

Information we get at the beginning of the conversation:	
How does this match?	

- The client's tone of voice towards the end:
  - ☐ understanding
  - ☐ angry
  - ☐ annoyed
  - ☐ joking
- The assistant's tone of voice towards the end:
  - ☐ understanding
  - ☐ polite
  - ☐ annoyed
  - ☐ unfriendly

Information we get at the end of the conversation:	
How does this match?	

Topic 16: An Inuit legend

52 Before you listen, remember what you know about Inuits and Aboriginal legends. Tick the correct boxes below. There is more than one correct answer.

a) The Inuit People …

- ☐ live in Australia.
- ☐ live on the North American continent.
- ☐ are also called Indians.
- ☐ are sometimes called Eskimos.

b) Legends …

- ☐ are stories.
- ☐ sometimes explain how the natural world works.
- ☐ tell of events that are said to have happened a long time ago.
- ☐ often have a message.

53 Now listen to the text. To get a general idea of what the text is about, complete the table below. Which myth does the story explain?

Track 11

Who?	
Where?	
When?	
What?	
Why?	
Myth?	

54 Listen to the passages from the text. Try to understand what the following expressions might mean. Explain them in your own words.

Track 12

a) to be on the prowl:

____

b) grunts and rasps:

____

c) to flare up (hope):

____

d) to trickle:

____

55 In the legend you learn a lot about Man's emotions. Here you have a list of different emotions he goes through at different stages of the story. Find the reason why he feels that way. You may listen to the text again.

Track 11

Emotions	Reasons
worried	*he worries that he will have to return to his family without food*
excited	
happy	
afraid	
sad	

56 In the story the characters are referred to as Man, Woman and Son. They are not given proper names or referred to as **a** man, **a** woman or **a** son. Explain why that is.

Topic 17: Strategien zum Hörverstehen

57 In diesem Kapitel hast du verschiedene Strategien verwendet, um Hörtexte besser zu verstehen oder Aufgaben leichter lösen zu können. Suche die Hörstrategien in den *Step up!*–Kästen des Kapitels und trage sie in die folgende Tabelle ein.

Du musst entscheiden, ob es sich um eine Strategie zum *pre-, while-* oder *post-listening* handelt oder ob sie dir hilft, unbekannte Wörter zu erschließen.

Listening-Strategies
Vor dem Hören: ➡ Vermutungen über den Text anstellen (mit Hilfe von Bildern, Überschrift, Aufgaben und Textsorte) (S. 36) ➡ ➡ ➡ ➡
Während des Hörens: ➡ Notizen machen: W-Fragen (S. 41) ➡ Notizen machen: Substantive … ➡ ➡
Wenn ich Wörter nicht verstehe: ➡
Nach dem (ersten) Hören: ➡ ➡

Words and spelling –
Wie du deinen Wortschatz und deine Rechtschreibung verbessern kannst

In diesem Kapitel dreht sich alles um den Wortschatz, denn ohne Wörter bist du im wahrsten Sinne des Wortes „sprachlos“. Du wirst hier sowohl auf bekannte, als auch auf (noch) unbekannte Wörter stoßen.

- Im Kapitel *Reading* gibt es bereits Informationen dazu, wie du mit **unbekannten Wörtern** umgehst (S. 2); damit solltest du also beginnen.
- Zu Beginn eines jeden *Topics* wird der **Grundwortschatz** eingeführt und dann in verschiedenen Übungsformen trainiert, die du auch gut auf den Lernwortschatz aus deinem Unterricht übertragen kannst.
- Sicherlich kennst du mittlerweile schon eine ganze Menge Arten und Wege des **Vokabellernens**. Besonders wichtig ist es, dass du regelmäßig übst. Es ist sinnvoller, jeden Tag über einen kurzen Zeitraum Vokabeln zu lernen, als einmal pro Woche oder vor einem Test eine ganze Stunde.
- Schwierige Wörter solltest du immer auch schriftlich üben. In den *Step up!*-Kästen dieses Kapitels findest du auch Hinweise zur **Schreibweise** sowie Möglichkeiten, den **Wortschatz umzuwälzen** und ihn somit zu **festigen**. Schließlich solltest du darauf achten, die Wörter nicht isoliert, sondern gemeinsam mit den Wörtern zu lernen, mit denen sie für gewöhnlich auftauchen (z. B. „do“ und „homework“, „make“ und „mistakes“ etc.).
- Zu manchen Aufgaben gibt es Hördateien, mit denen du auch deine **Aussprache** verbessern kannst. Übe, indem du dir die Aufnahmen mehrfach anhörst, um dir die richtige Aussprache einzuprägen. Versuche, sie auch nachzusprechen und höre sie dir schließlich nochmals zur Korrektur an.
- Am Ende des Kapitels kannst du dir eine Übersicht über alle Strategien, die du kennengelernt hast, erstellen, um deine Fertigkeiten im Bereich „words and spelling“ zu verbessern.

Topic 18: Peers and friends

Step up!

Kollokationen …

… sind Wörter, die häufig zusammen auftreten, z. B. *to take an exam*.

- Deutsche Kollokationen können sich von englischen unterscheiden (z. B. „Es macht mir Spaß“ → “*It is fun*”; “~~*It makes me fun*~~”).
- Lerne Kollokationen, um Fehler zu vermeiden, aber auch um deinen Ausdruck zu variieren (z. B. *pitch black* anstatt *very dark*). ■

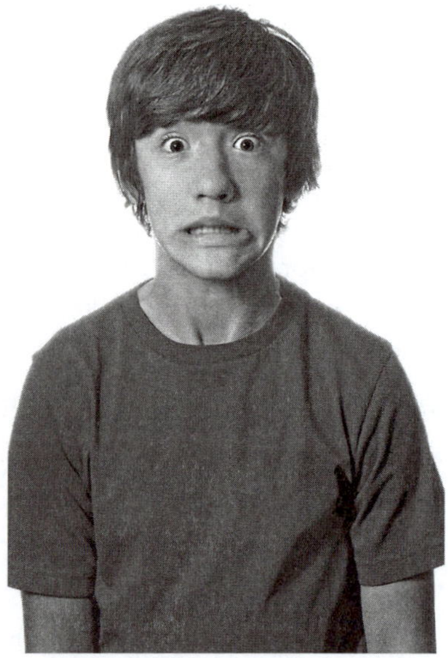

58 Track 13 Listen to the short text and read along to find out how the words are pronounced. Then read the short text carefully once again and underline all the words that mean “very”. Note them down in the collocation used here. The first one has been done for you.

Peter’s highly unusual behaviour annoyed his classmates intensely. He used to shout really loudly whenever he said something. And what he said was usually downright stupid, too. We all criticised him strongly and some students even started bullying him, but still he didn’t change his behaviour. Today, I strongly believe that he just couldn’t help it and I am deeply sorry for making his life at school utterly miserable.

highly unusual – …

____

____

____

____

____

____

____

____

59 Read the expressions in the box and find antonyms (≠) for the words below. There are two more expressions than you need.

Step up!

Antonyme
Antonyme sind Wörter mit gegenteiliger Bedeutung (z. B. *happy* und *sad*).
Du lernst Vokabeln leichter, wenn du diese immer wieder neu sortierst und umwälzt. Überlege dir bei Wörtern, die du lernst, ob du andere Wörter kennst, die vielleicht das Gleiche oder auch das Gegenteil bedeuten. ■

to break up a friendship • a close friend • to make friends with sb • a true friend • to keep in touch with sb • a circle of friends

a) a casual acquaintance ≠ ____________________

b) to form a friendship ≠ ____________________

c) a fair-weather friend ≠ ____________________

d) to lose contact with sb ≠ ____________________

The two expressions not needed are

- ____________________
- ____________________

60 Translate all the expressions from the previous exercise into German. Underline the expressions that are different in German.

to break up a friendship	
a casual acquaintance	
a close friend	
a fair-weather friend	
to form a friendship	
to keep in touch with sb	
to lose contact with sb	
to make friends with sb	
my circle of friends	

61 Do you remember when you were new at your school? How did friendships develop then? Write a short text of about 100 words in which you use at least five of the expressions from the previous exercise.

You may start like this: *When I changed from primary to secondary school ...*

Topic 19: Describing characters

62 Find 10 adjectives (from left to right or from top to bottom) that can be used to describe a person's character. Then write those words down in the table on the next page. Decide if the words describe a positive or a negative character trait. Two adjectives have already been marked for you.

V	R	T	C	L	E	V	E	R	U	I	P	D	E	X
S	E	N	S	I	T	I	V	E	E	R	B	I	M	E
O	L	K	S	D	F	L	D	L	Y	R	C	N	K	B
A	I	S	R	T	W	U	N	D	I	N	K	G	D	E
C	K	P	E	S	S	I	M	I	S	T	I	C	S	K
Z	E	O	N	V	R	B	T	H	A	P	P	Y	X	I
F	A	O	G	C	U	K	A	B	K	E	L	W	E	N
R	B	R	O	A	I	N	S	E	K	U	R	E	S	D
I	L	A	N	I	U	E	W	T	I	O	U	S	E	T
E	R	A	E	B	O	R	I	N	G	K	O	S	K	L
N	J	N	T	L	C	V	U	L	I	B	C	N	B	S
D	D	G	I	L	S	O	R	E	L	I	A	B	L	E
L	B	R	H	O	P	U	G	L	Y	M	Z	N	F	G
Y	R	Y	K	D	M	S	A	R	Z	O	B	E	I	N
A	B	S	U	L	R	V	S	J	E	K	T	K	I	L

positive trait	negative trait
sensitive	nervous

63 The words below are opposites of the words from the previous exercise. Find the pairs and complete the list below.
Then add the German translations. If necessary, look them up in a dictionary.

calm • interesting • stupid • relaxed • unfriendly • cruel • unreliable • sad • insensitive • rich • pretty • optimistic

Step up!
Im Englischen gibt es verschiedene **Vorsilben**, die ein Adjektiv ins Gegenteil verkehren, z. B.
- *il-legal*
- *ir-regular*
- *im-polite*
- *in-tolerant*
- *un-pleasant*
- *dis-honest* ■

English		German	
positive trait	**negative trait**	***positive Eigenschaft***	***negative Eigenschaft***
sensitive	insensitive	sensibel, einfühlsam	gefühllos, taktlos
	nervous		

positive trait	**negative trait**	***positive Eigenschaft***	***negative Eigenschaft***

64 Complete the sentences using words from your list.

a) Sam always tells the same stories and he only ever wants to talk about football. He is really a very ______________________ person to talk to.

b) I can't believe how ______________________ she is. She doesn't understand the simplest things and she will do anything you tell her to do without thinking.

c) Terry really believes that he will pass his exam. He hasn't revised at all and he's missed quite a few lessons, but he is still very ______________________ that he will do just fine.

d) Sally wanted to pick me up for the party at 7 pm. We had to be at Maria's at 7.30 but at 7.20 she still hadn't arrived. When I called her, she was still getting dressed. I just can't believe how ______________________ she is.

e) Our teacher got really mad at us when he realized that none of us had done our homework. I don't think I've ever seen him so ______________________. He shouted at us for about 5 minutes.

f) Mr Gonzalez can't stand cats. Whenever he can, he throws stones at them. He told his neighbour he would kill their cat if it ever came into their garden again. He is really a very ______________________ man.

65 Use at least six of the adjectives that you learned in this topic to describe yourself briefly:

Topic 20: The fence

66 Complete the table below by adding the words from the same word family. Sometimes you can find more than one noun or adjective in a word family. Some boxes stay empty. Find a German caption for the word field.

Step up!
Die Arbeit mit **Wortfamilien** ist eine weitere gute Möglichkeit, den Wortschatz umzuwälzen und zu erweitern. Wenn du den **Wortstamm** (z. B. *il-legal-ly*) kennst, ist es vergleichsweise leicht, weitere Wörter davon abzuleiten. ■

immigration, discriminated (against), immigrated, nationality, hope, discrimination, racism, majority, smuggle, smuggler, minority, different, immigrant, hopeless, differ, racist, nation, hopeful

verb	noun(s)	adjective(s)	*Wortfeld*
		racist	*Rassismus*
(to) immigrate to			
(to) discriminate against			
	hope		
	difference		
		major	
		minor	*Minderheit*
		national	
	smuggling		

67 a) Leaving their home country

Fill in the missing prepositions. Then mark the reasons for leaving one's home country and translate them into German.

> **Step up!**
> **Präpositionen** (*of, on, from, in, about, etc.*) stellen oft ein Problem dar. Lerne sie bei den Vokabeln immer gleich mit, da manchmal Unterschiede zum Deutschen auftreten können, z. B. „**unter** etwas leiden" aber *to suffer* ***from*** *something.* ■

There are many reasons ______ people to leave their home country. Some leave because they live ______ poverty and they hope ______ a better future in a different country. Others suffer ______ discrimination, and some people even fear ______ their lives.

Reasons for leaving:

- ____________________
- ____________________
- ____________________
- ____________________

b) Getting to another country

Match the two halves of the sentences.

A They cross	a Green Card in the USA.	**1**	**A**	
B They climb	a smuggler to smuggle them into the US.	**2**	**B**	
C They pay	a border illegally.	**3**	**C**	
D We seek	asylum in Europe.	**4**	**D**	
E We apply for	a fence at the US-Mexico border.	**5**	**E**	

c) **Living in another country**

Match the two halves of the sentences.

A My dad was an illegal	two cultures.	**1**
B He did unskilled	work.	**2**
C Many children grow up in	discrimination.	**3**
D They grow up	immigrant.	**4**
E Because of their background they often face	bilingually, many of them speaking Spanish and English.	**5**

A	
B	
C	
D	
E	

68 Mrs Ramirez, an immigrant from Mexico, is interviewed for an American newspaper. Read the interview and use expressions from the previous exercises to complete the text.

INTERVIEWER: Good morning, Mrs Ramirez. Thank you for your time and for sharing your story with us. Why don't you start by telling us what brought you to San Diego.

MRS RAMIREZ: I was born in a little village in Mexico. We lived in poverty there. Our situation was really desperate because in Mexico there is a lot of crime and we often feared for ________________ ________________. Our children were of course much younger then. We wanted a better future for them. That's why we decided to leave Mexico.

INTERVIEWER: But it isn't easy to cross the US-Mexico border – not with the tight controls and the fence.

MRS RAMIREZ: Yes, that was the hardest part. We tried to cross ______________ ______________ illegally a few times. But we were always caught by the border patrol and sent back. Finally we decided to pay a ______________ to take us over the border. In the dead of night we walked to the fence and he showed us a spot where to ________________ the fence. My family was lucky. We made it and were hidden on the American side when the border control came. But ten people in our group were caught that night.

INTERVIEWER: What is life like here in San Diego?

MRS RAMIREZ: Now we are really happy. Two years ago we finally became US Americans but it took a lot to get there. First we took on any kind of farm work we could get. It was frustrating because my husband is a mechanic and I am a nurse, but we could only find ______________ work. And we were always afraid of being discovered and sent back to Mexico.

INTERVIEWER: What was it like for your children?

MRS RAMIREZ: They went to school here, so they had to ________ ______ in two cultures. They were often ________________ against because their parents are ________________. They often cried at home and didn't want to return to school. But we explained how important education is. As a result they have grown up ______________, which is an important advantage for them because it will help them to find a job.

INTERVIEWER: Does that mean you're happy with your decision to leave your home country?

MRS RAMIREZ: Absolutely. Of course, I do miss my home and my family, but we've built a good life for ourselves here. The first couple of years were really hard, though. But now I can even send some money to my family back in Mexico from time to time. Sometimes we still have to ______________ discrimination but in our neighbourhood the __________________ of the people are Hispanics, so it feels a bit like home.

INTERVIEWER: Thank you for your time, Mrs Ramirez.

Topic 21: Feelings and emotions

69 a) Look at the pictures and describe the people with adjectives that express feelings and emotions.

____

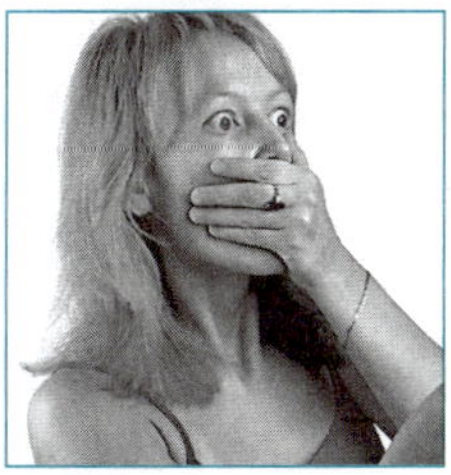

____

____

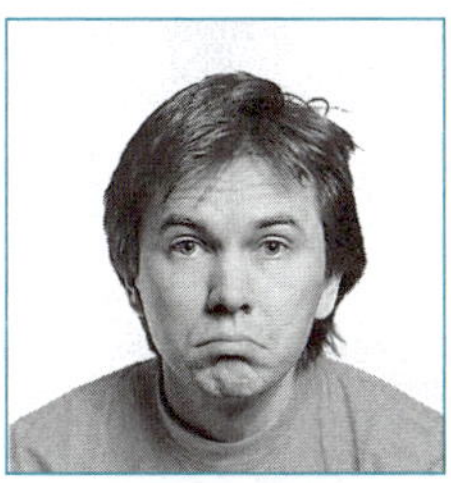

____

____

b) Complete the mind map with adjectives. Add prepositions where needed.

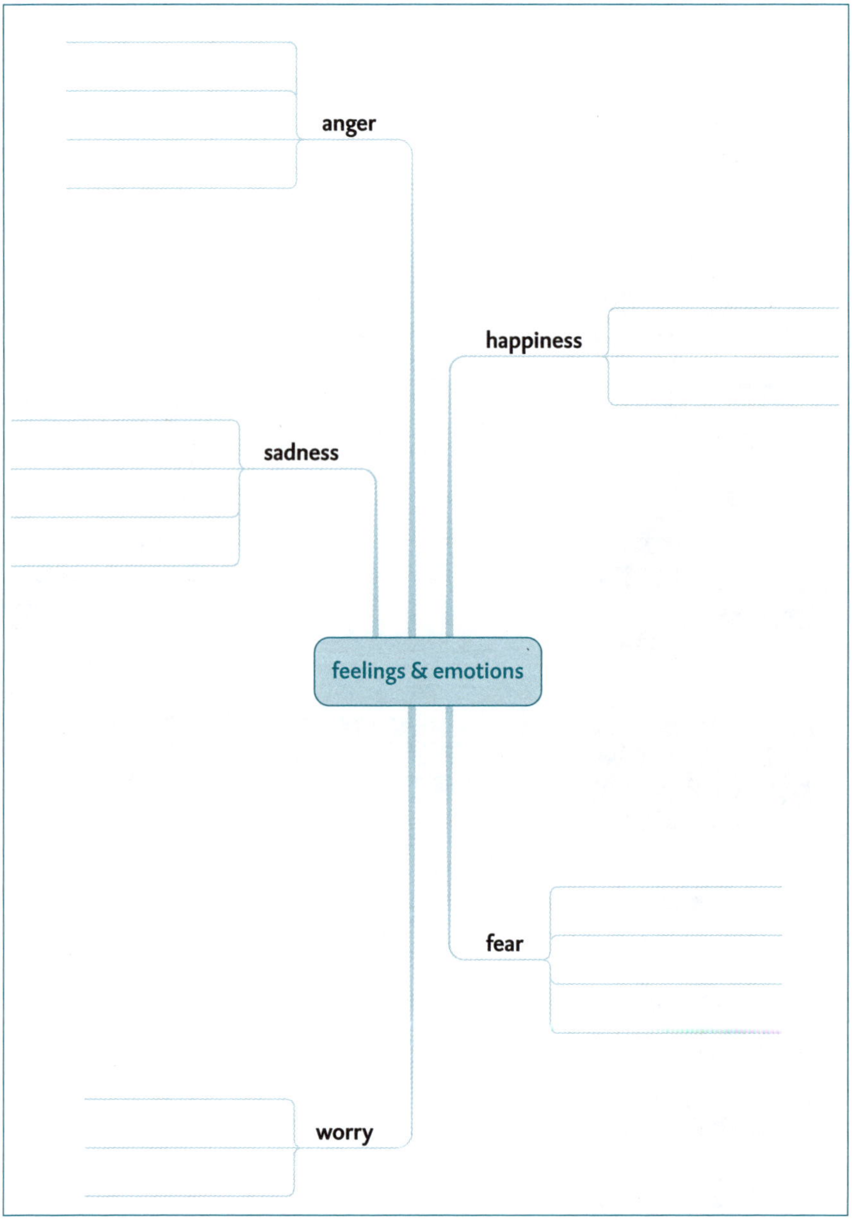

70 Read the following phrases. Decide where they fit in the following mind map.

for fear of • (to) be worried sick • with a heavy heart • (to) cry with happiness at sth • out of fear • a face glows with happiness • the anger over sth grows • (to) lose one's temper • (to) be trembling with fear

Step up!

Mindmaps eignen sich hervorragend, um Wörter aus einem bestimmten **Themenfeld** zusammenzustellen. So hast du alle Ausdrücke, die du zu einem Themenfeld kennst oder noch lernen willst, auf einmal im Blick. ■

71 Read the following phrases. Then put them in the table below.

> ~~dissatisfied with sb/sth~~ • excited about • deeply disappointed with sb • madly jealous of • nervous about • embarrassed at/by • sorry about sth/for sb • enthusiastic about • to my regret • to go green with envy • ashamed of • upset about

Step up!

Achte darauf, dass Wörter, die im Englischen auf *-ful* enden nur mit einem *-l* geschrieben werden, z. B. *regretful, fearful, hopeful.* ■

disappointment	*dissatisfied with sb/sth, ...*
embarrassment	
jealousy	
regret	
excitement	

72 Replace the phrase in brackets with one of the collocations from the box to complete the sentences. There are two more phrases than you need.

> really sad • madly in love • extremely pleased • deeply disappointed • deeply concerned • terribly angry • terribly frightened

a) She is ______________________ (very afraid) of spiders.

b) He is ______________________ (very happy) that he still got tickets for the concert.

c) I'm ______________________ (very unhappy) that you're leaving.

d) They are ______________________ (very worried) about their son.

e) They are ______________________ (very mad) at their teacher.

73 Decide which of the three words fits best in the sentence.

a)

❶ smiling • glowing • going	❷ sick • ill • extremely
❸ deeply • terribly • extremely	❹ cry • shout • call

Mary has just got the results of her exams and now her face is ❶ ________ with happiness. Last night she was worried ❷ ________ for fear of the results but at the moment she is ❸ ________ pleased with herself. She could easily ❹ ________ with happiness.

b)

❶ crazily • bitterly • madly	❷ highly • deeply • madly
❸ grew • rose • glowed	❹ got • caught • lost

When Sue saw her boyfriend with her best friend, she was ❶ ________ jealous. She was too ❷ ________ disappointed with both of them to say anything. But on her way home her anger ❸ ________ and she finally ❹ ________ her temper and called her boyfriend.

c)

❶ sadness • regret • anger	❷ heavy • aching • sorry
❸ madly • deeply • utterly	❹ green • blue • red

To my great ❶ ________ my favourite band split up. Whenever I listen to their last CD, I do so with a ❷ ________ heart. I'm ❸ ________ depressed by their decision and could go ❹ ________ with envy because my sister went to their last concert.

Topic 22: US history

74 Put the letters together correctly to find the English words. The sentences help you to find the correct words. The first one has already been filled in.

a) The British settlers fought for it in a war:

independence

E P E I N N C E D N E D

b) Christopher Columbus was one:

____

R E L X E O R P

c) At first the Native Americans helped them:

____

E T S E R L T S

d) The English people who sailed to America on the Mayflower:

____

S M I L P I R G

e) Another word for illness:

____

S E I E D S A

f) To continue to live or exist:

____

U S R I V E V

g) It is celebrated on Thanksgiving:

____

A T R V S H E

h) Massachussetts was the first one and there were thirteen in the beginning:

____

N O Y C L O

i) The Native Americans and the settlers had different ones:

____

N O T A I D R I S T

j) To start something, such as a town or an institution:

____

F O U D N

75 Odd one out. Find the word or phrase that cannot be used to form a collocation with the head word and cross it out. Then use the three collocations that remain to write example sentences for each of them. The first one (a) has been done for you.

a) **settlers** →

early	first	to found	~~to institute~~

- The Pilgrims were early settlers from Europe.
- The first settlers in America had a really hard life.
- Settlers founded this colony.

b) **independence** →

to declare	to win	difficult	hard-won

- __________
- __________
- __________

c) **disease** →

to catch	to spread	to treat	to give

- __________
- __________
- __________

d) **to survive** →

poorly	hardly	to struggle	to manage

- __________
- __________
- __________

e) **colony** →

to found	small	overseas	to take

- __________
- __________
- __________

76 Fill in the missing words in the following text. Use the collocations and words you've learned from the previous exercises.

In 1620 the first ______________ from Europe ______________ a colony they called Plymouth. Unfortunately, they spread ______________ which the Native Americans weren't able to ______________. In autumn, the ______________ only brought in a poor ______________ and many died of hunger and cold during the first winter.

Others managed to ______________. They fought with the Native Americans over the land and later against the British for ______________. Today, the Native Americans are trying to keep their centuries-old ______________ alive.

Topic 23: British and American English

77 Track 14

Some words are spelled differently in British and American English.
Read the following rules and find more examples for each category. Then listen to the track for more ideas. You will hear the American pronunciation.

Step up!
In der Regel hast du die Wahl zwischen ***British*** und ***American English***. Du solltest dich aber für eine Variante entscheiden und dich durchgängig an die entsprechenden Regeln halten. ■

a) British English words that end in *-re* often end in *-er* in American English.

British English	American English
centre	center

b) British English words that end in *-our* often end in *-or* in American English.

British English	American English
colour	color

c) Verbs that end in [-aiz] are usually spelled *-ise* in British English and always *-ize* in American English.

British English	American English
to organise	to organize

d) Nouns that end in [-ẹn̊(t)s] are spelled *-ence* in British English and *-ense* in American English.

British English	American English
defence	defense

e) In verbs in British English the final *-l* is doubled in the *-ed* or *-ing* forms. In American English there is only one *-l*.

British English	American English
to marvel, marvelled	to marvel, marveled

78 Sometimes they use different words in British and American English. Read the texts and replace the American English words with British English ones. You can listen to the texts in both British and American English afterwards.

Track 15

At school

a) This morning there was a message on the ____________ *(bulletin board)* announcing a ____________ *(field day)* for next Friday. I guess I'll play ____________ *(soccer)* then.

b) When I entered the building, I heard the ____________ *(janitor)* talking to the ____________ *(principal)*. He complained that the students left too much ____________ *(garbage)* on the floor and did not use the ____________ *(trash cans)*.

c) Just look at my _______________ *(schedule)*. Each day starts with __________ *(Math)*. How horrible! I need a _______________ *(vacation)* already!

d) My cousin used to have very bad ___________ *(grades)*. Then he changed to a very expensive _________________ *(private school)* and this ____________ *(grade)* he is doing much better.

Traffic

e) We should have taken the ________________ *(subway)* to go ____________________ *(downtown)*.

f) The traffic on the _______________ *(highway)* is very heavy again. I wish I had a ___________ *(motorcycle)*. I'd be much quicker then.

At the shopping mall

g) I'm hungry. Can't we stop here for some ______________ *(French fries)*?

h) ______________ *(Mom)*, can we buy some ___________________ *(potato chips)* before we go to the ____________________ *(movies)*?

79 Track 16

Pronunciation is different in British and American English. Listen to the following statements. You are going to hear each statement twice. Decide which is British and which American. The first one has been done for you.

1

a) British English ☐
b) American English ☑

2

a) British English ☐
b) American English ☐

3

a) British English ☐
b) American English ☐

4

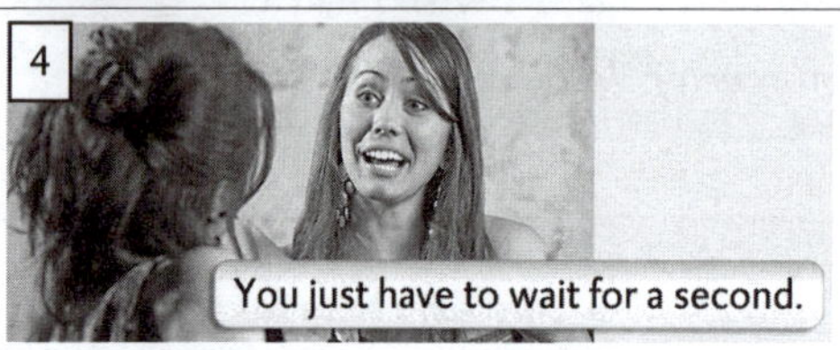

a) British English ☐
b) American English ☐

5

a) British English ☐
b) American English ☐

6

a) British English ☐
b) American English ☐

Topic 24: Strategien zum Wortschatz

80 In diesem Kapitel hast du verschiedenen Strategien verwendet, um den Wortschatz zu festigen und zu erweitern. Suche die Strategien in den *Step up!*-Kästen des Kapitels und trage sie in die folgende Tabelle ein.

Learning-Strategies
Vokabeln lernen: ➡ jeden Tag 5-10 Minuten (S. 57) ➡ mündlich und schriftlich üben ➡ Vokabelkasten oder -heft ➡ Lernsoftware ➡ ➡ ➡
Wortschatz erweitern: ➡ ➡ ➡
Rechtschreibregeln: ➡ Endsilbe -ful mit einem „l", z.B. hopeful (S. 72) ➡ British vs. American English (S. 77/78) -re → -er -our → -ise → -ence → -ll- →

Mediation –
Wie du deine Kompetenz zur Sprachmittlung verbessern kannst

In diesem Kapitel trainierst du, wie du Informationen **vom Deutschen ins Englische** und vom **Englischen ins Deutsche** überträgst. Die Fähigkeit zwischen zwei Sprachen zu mitteln ist eine sehr wichtige, da Verständigung zwischen Menschen, die nicht dieselbe Sprache sprechen, nur auf diese Weise möglich ist.

- **Sprachmittlung ist jedoch keine Übersetzung**, also keine wortwörtliche Übertragung von einer Sprache in die andere. Stattdessen „(ver-)mittelst" du die Inhalte, die in dem konkreten Zusammenhang wichtig sind, und zwar so, dass dein Gegenüber dich auch versteht.
- Das bedeutet z. B., dass du dir bei der Sprachmittlung auch Gedanken machen musst, welche **kulturellen Informationen** du eventuell ergänzen musst, weil dein Gegenüber nicht über dieses Wissen verfügt. So müsstest du z. B., wenn du über typisch deutsche Festtagsbräuche oder regionale Traditionen sprichst, zusätzliche Informationen hinzufügen, etwa, woher der Brauch kommt oder wie er gefeiert wird.
- Bevor du mit der Sprachmittlung beginnst, musst du dir immer überlegen, **mit wem** du sprichst bzw. an wen du schreibst und **mit welcher Absicht**. Die Antworten auf diese Fragen geben dir dann darüber Aufschluss, wie du dich ausdrücken musst und welche Informationen in dieser Situation wichtig, weniger wichtig oder gar überflüssig sind.

Topic 25: Going shopping

81 Before starting with a mediation exercise, you should always make sure that it is clear to you what you are expected to do.
Read the task in exercise 82 and look at the pictures. Take some notes in German.

> **Step up!**
> **Vor der Sprachmittlung** ist stets zu beachten:
> - Mit wem ***(who)*** sprichst du?
> - Wie sprichst du mit deinem Gegenüber bzw. wie schreibst du an diese Person ***(choice of words)***?
> - Mit welcher Absicht ***(purpose)*** mittelst du?
> - Welche Informationen aus dem Text sind wichtig ***(relevant aspects)***? Welche kannst du weglassen? ■

- *Ziel/Absicht*: ______________________________

  ____
- *Für wen*: eine Cousine aus Amerika
- *Wortwahl*: ______________________________

82 **A visitor from the US**

> **Step up!**
> Bei kürzeren Texten ist es häufig sinnvoll, kurze Erklärungen zu ergänzen, damit der Inhalt für andere verständlich wird. ■

One day, you and your cousin from the US, who is staying with you during the summer holidays, go shopping together. While you are walking past the shops, she sees a lot of signs which she cannot make sense of. Explain to her the meaning of the different signs. The first one (a) has been done for you.

a) 

If you buy three pairs of shoes, you'll get the cheapest pair for free.

b) 
Sammeln Sie Punkte!
Nur heute und morgen:
5-fach Punkte auf
ihren Einkauf mit der
Shopping Card.

c) 
Zutritt
unter
18
Jahren
unter-
sagt

d) 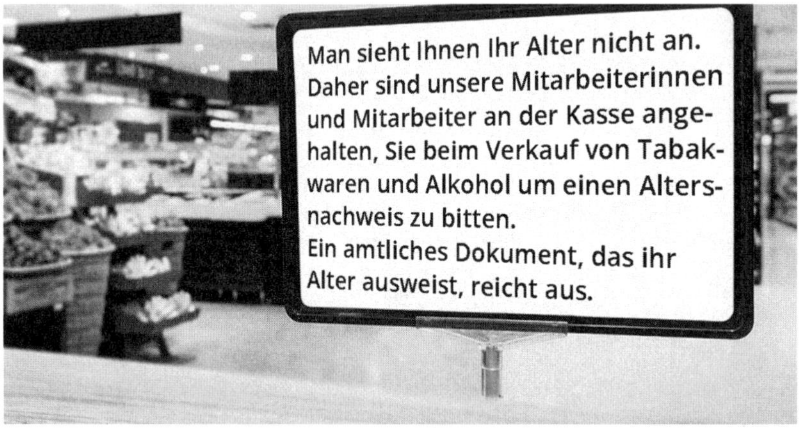
Man sieht Ihnen Ihr Alter nicht an.
Daher sind unsere Mitarbeiterinnen und Mitarbeiter an der Kasse angehalten, Sie beim Verkauf von Tabakwaren und Alkohol um einen Altersnachweis zu bitten.
Ein amtliches Dokument, das ihr Alter ausweist, reicht aus.

e) 
Wochenendangebot:
1 Brot,
10 Brötchen
nur
4,99 EUR

Topic 26: Taking part in an exchange

83 A warm welcome

Some English pupils are at your school for a week and one of them, Tanita, is staying with you and your family. In order to welcome the English guests, your headmaster gives a speech. Tanita does not understand everything and asks you about some things.

a) Before listening to the text, take some notes in German.

- *Ziel/Absicht*: Verständnisprobleme beheben, Informationen einer deutschsprachigen Rede auf Englisch zusammenfassen
- *Für wen*: ____
- *Wortwahl*: ____
- *Wichtige Aspekte*: *Unterstreiche dir in diesem Fall die Schlüsselwörter in Tanitas Fragen (Teilaufgabe b).*

Track 17

b) Now listen to the speech and answer Tanita's questions in English.

TANITA: What does he say? There are 300 pupils here? That's not true.

YOU: ____

TANITA: And what does he say about Mrs Smith?

YOU: ____

TANITA: And what about the T-shirt that she got? I could see the pictures on the front and lots of names on the back. Who signed it?

YOU: ______

TANITA: I think I understood what he said about the programme, but then at the end he said what we should take home. Will we get T-shirts too?

YOU: ______

84 The little brother

Your little brother is in the first year at school. He shows Tanita a picture of him on his first day and tells her about it. He does not speak English, so you have to mediate between them. Use your own words without looking at a dictionary or the internet.

Step up!

Übertragung von Informationen

Bei **landestypischen Begriffen** hilft in der Regel eine einfache Übertragung nicht. Hier musst du zusätzliche Informationen ergänzen, um den Inhalt für andere verständlich zu machen. ■

BROTHER: *Schau mal, Tanita, das bin ich am ersten Schultag. Da war ich sehr nervös, aber alle waren sehr nett, vor allem meine Lehrerin.*

YOU: He says that on this picture you can see him on his first day at school. ...

TANITA: The picture looks really nice, but what is that thing you're holding?

YOU: ______

BROTHER: *Aber das ist doch meine Schultüte. Anscheinend weiß sie nicht, was das ist. Erklär es ihr doch mal.*

YOU: ______

TANITA: OK. I've never heard of that. Was there anything inside?

YOU:

BROTHER: *Ja, es waren viele Süßigkeiten, Farbstifte und ein Stundenplan drin. Jetzt muss ich aber meine Hausaufgaben machen. Tschüß, Tanita.*

YOU:

TANITA: Yeah. Bye.

Topic 27: A visit to Chicago

85 Before the trip

You and your mum want to go on a trip to Chicago. Before leaving, your mum wants you to contact the hotel via email and ask for advice on some important issues.

> **Step up!**
> **Überflüssiges weglassen**
> Überlege genau, **welche Informationen** du mitteln musst und welche für den Adressaten unwichtig sind. ■

a) Look at your mum's questions. First mark important keywords. Then write the part of your email in which you ask the questions in English.

- MUM: „Wo kriegt man denn einen Stadtplan her? Meinst du, die haben da einen im Hotel an der Rezeption?"
- MUM: „Kannst du bitte auch fragen, ob es ein Tagesticket für Bus und Bahn gibt und wie viel das kostet?"
- MUM: „Mich interessiert noch, wo die nächste U-Bahn-Station ist. Kann man dort dann Tickets kaufen oder ist das im Hotel möglich?"
- MUM: „Und frag bitte noch, was sie Touristen als Hauptattraktion empfehlen."
- MUM: „Außerdem möchte ich wissen, wie das Wetter nächste Woche in Chicago wird und ob es dort oft regnet."

You can start like this:

I'm afraid I've got quite a few questions before our stay at your hotel. Would you be so kind to answer them?
1 Is it possible to get a city map at reception?
2 …

b) The hotel wrote an email back. Mark the information you need to answer your mum's questions.

New Message

To meandmymumonholiday@web.com Cc Bcc

Subject Q&A visit

Dear future guests,

We are looking forward to welcoming you at our hotel.
In the following, we would like to answer the questions you asked in your email: First of all, you will be pleased to know that there will be a city map and a CTA system map (that shows all train and bus routes in Chicago) waiting for you at reception when you arrive. For using public transport, we recommend a three-day CTA Pass for $ 20, which you cannot buy at our reception, unfortunately, but which you can get at the nearest train station (just 300 yards down the road).
One of the main attractions here is the Chicago Architecture Foundation River Cruise. It is great to get a first impression of the city and the guides will tell you loads of interesting things about the buildings along the Chicago River. You will also learn something about the city's history.
The weather in Chicago will be nice next week. However, the weather forecast said that there is a possibility of slight rain on Thursday and Friday – which can happen all the time during this season, I am afraid.
I hope I was able to answer all your questions. Do not hesitate to ask again if not. We are at your service here 24/7.

Sincerely,
Edith Moon

Reception Manager
The Chicago Grand

Send

Write down what you tell your mum in about 100 words:

____

____

____

____

____

____

86 At the hotel

You and your mum are staying in a hotel on the 17th floor. Your mum is worried about your safety in case of fire. In your room you find the information sheet below and you tell your mum what it says to calm her down.

Step up!

Vorbereitung der Sprachmittlung

- Markiere dir wichtige Stellen im Text.
- Überlege, welche Stellen dir Schwierigkeiten bereiten könnten, z. B. Wortbedeutungen.
- Nutze Worterschließungsstrategien (z. B. *word formation*).
- Schlage notfalls Wörter im Wörterbuch nach. Beschränke dich aber auf einige wenige, da das Nachschlagen sehr viel Zeit in Anspruch nimmt. ■

a) Read the information sheet on the next page carefully. Underline the relevant passages that you need to explain the hotel's safety measures to your mother (see b).

FIRE ACTION!!!

IF YOU DISCOVER A FIRE

1. *Operate the nearest fire alarm. The emergency plan will tell you where to find it.*
2. *Dial 911 to call the fire department. Tell them who you are, what has happened and where you are. Don't hang up before being told to do so.*
3. *If possible, tackle the fire using the appliances provided. The emergency plan will tell you where the fire extinguishers are. Be careful not to endanger yourself or others when doing so.*

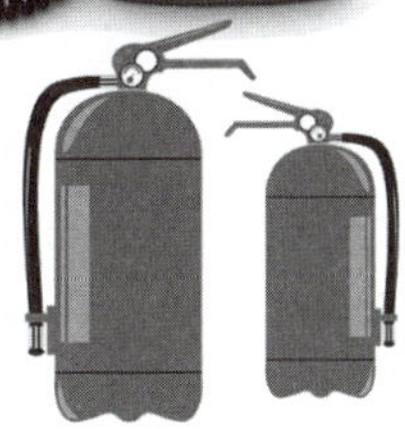

IF YOU HEAR THE FIRE ALARM

4. *Leave the building by the nearest available exit. Follow the green signs.*
5. *If possible, help others who need assistance.*
6. *Use the stairs. Do not use the lift!*
7. *Close all doors behind you.*
8. *Report to the person in charge of the assembly point.*

CAUTION

9. *If smoke is heavy in the corridors, it may be safer to stay in your room. Close the door and place a wet towel at the base of the door.*
   A rescue team will come in less than 5 minutes.

ABOVE ALL: REMAIN CALM

b) Write down in German how you would explain the safety measures to your mother. Write about 150–200 words. Tell her:

- what to do if she discovers a fire,
- how to find the quickest way out,
- what to do if you can't leave your room,
- what to do when you've left the building successfully.

Topic 28: Camp Cooper

In your next summer holidays you would like to go to an international summer camp. So you have searched the internet for some interesting offers. You have found the following website.

*** only a few days left til camp !! ******* only a few days left til camp !! ***

Camp Cooper is a traditional overnight summer camp based in Scotland, for international & British campers aged 7–17. Camp Cooper is the UK's leading American-style summer camp.
Campers create a personalised summer programme designed to suit their interests. We offer exceptional tuition in English, sport, dance, circus skills, journalism, mountain biking, art, swimming, music, film-making, outdoor adventure, performing arts, football and tennis. At Camp Cooper, we actively encourage campers to develop independence, confidence and leadership. We focus on forming friendships, inspiring creativity, building life skills and having fun. Parents rated our Camp 9.5 out of 10 and 100% of them would recommend us to a friend!

** Quick facts *** Quick facts *** Quick facts *** Quick facts **

* 10 hours of English language tuition available per week
* Professionally-led activities including sports, art, drama, dance, mountain biking, media & outdoor adventure!
* 1:4 staff to camper ratio
* 2,4 & 6-week sessions available,
* For ages 7-17
* Exciting evening events including talent shows, music festivals, Hawaiian luaus, colour competitions and camp fires
* New Activities, Friendships & Experiences

*** only a few days left til camp !! ******* only a few days left til camp !! ***

Camp Cooper, http://www.internationalsummercampuk.com/

87 Make sure that you know the meaning of some important words. Find the most suitable German translation for each of the following words and underline it in the dictionary entries below. Look closely at the context in which they are given in the text. The first one (a) has been done for you.

Step up!

Verwendung des Wörterbuchs
Wenn du in einem zweisprachigen Wörterbuch nachschlägst, findest du meist **viele verschiedene Bedeutungen** für ein Wort. Betrachte immer den **Kontext**, in dem das Wort vorkommt, um die richtige Bedeutung und Übersetzung auszuwählen. ■

a) **tuition** [tju:ˈɪʃn; US auch tʊ-] s

n **1.** *(besonders Einzel-, Privat)* **Unterricht** *m*
2. *besonders* US
a) (SCHULE) **Schulgeld** *n*
b) (UNIV) **Studiengebühren** *pl*

b) **ratio** [ˈreɪʃɪəʊ; US auch -ʃəʊ] pl -os s

n **1.** (MATH) *etc* **Verhältnis** *n*
2. (MATH) **Quotient** *m*
3. (WIRTSCH) **Wertverhältnis** *n* **zwischen Gold und Silber**
4. (TECH) **Übersetzungsverhältnis** *n (eines Getriebes)*

c) **suit** [su:t; BE auch sju:t]

v **1. passen**
2. *(Kleider, Farben etc.)* **stehen**
3. *besonders* BE *(gut tun)* **bekommen** *(meist verneinte Sätze)*

d) **exceptional** [ikˈsepʃənl]

adj **1. hervorragend**
2. auffällig
3. ungewöhnlich

e) **encourage** [inˈkʌridʒ; US -ˈɜ:r-]

v **1.** *(to encourage sth)* **fördern**
2. *(to encourage sb)* **ermutigen**
3. (SPORT) **anfeuern**

f) **develop** [diˈveləp]

v **1. entstehen**
2. *sich (aus etw) (zu etw)* **entwickeln**
3. *(Fehler etc.)* **auftreten**

g) **confidence** [ˈkɒnfɪdəns; US ˈkɑ:n-]

n **1. Zuversicht**
2. Vertrauen
3. Selbstbewusstsein

h) **recommend** [rekəˈmend]

v **1. (weiter)empfehlen**
2. *(jmd für etw)* **vorschlagen** *(z. B. Beförderung)*
3. befürworten

88 Now tell your parents about the website. The following guidelines will help you to pass on all the important information to them:

Tell them
- where the camp will be,
- who will take part,
- how long it lasts,
- some activities that are offered,
- what you can do in the evening,
- what is important to the organisation,
- what parents think about the camp.

89 **Finding out more**

Your parents are quite happy with your idea of going to an international camp. However, they would like to know some more details before making a final decision. So they have made a list of questions they would like to have some answers to. Use that list to prepare for a phone call to the people organising the summer camp. Write down the questions you want to ask in English.

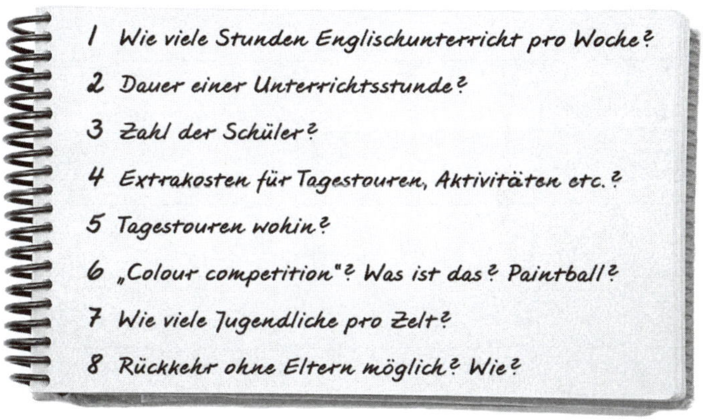

1. ______________________________
2. ______________________________
3. ______________________________
4. ______________________________
5. ______________________________
6. ______________________________
7. ______________________________
8. ______________________________

90 Informing your parents

Track 18

a) Listen to the phone call and take some notes in order to be able to answer your parents' questions. You can use your parents' list or your own notes to add the answers given on the phone. Take your notes in English or in German. If you have problems understanding the phone call, listen to it again. You can also stop the recording to take notes. If necessary, you may read through the transcript on page 205/206.

b) Use your notes to write down what you would say to your parents.

Topic 29: Immigration to the US

91 Help!

a) Your class is cooperating with an American class. Read the e-mail which an American student has sent to you.

New Message

To mastablasta_finn@tmail.de Cc Bcc

Subject immigration to US

Hi there

I hope you're all doing fine. We just returned from the autumn break and school is as tough as ever!
Last week we started a new project in our History class. We are talking about immigration to the US. Mara, Michelle, Paul and I, we focus on German immigrants in the 19th century. We have found a German website which seems interesting, but we have some problems understanding the details. We tried using a translation program but the results don't make a lot of sense.
We now know that the website is about people from Bavaria and have learned some interesting words, like a "Dampfschiff" is a steamer and "hygienische Verhältnisse" is sanitary conditions, but hey, that doesn't really help us. Could you please read the website and tell us

- how emigrants from Bavaria got to the US?
- what made life on the ships so hard?
- how the journey by ship changed in the 19th century?

Thanks a lot and say hello to everybody.

Yours
Tom

Send

In the e-mail Tom asks three specific questions he has about the information. Note down in German what he wants to know.

Tom wants to know ...	***Tom will wissen ...***
... how emigrants from Bavaria got to the US.	...
... what made life on the ships so hard.	...
... how the journey by ship changed in the 19th century?	...

b) Read the information about the harbor *("Zum Hafen")* and the voyage *("Überfahrt")* and mark the information that you need to answer Tom's questions.

Auswanderung aus Bayern nach Amerika

Zum Hafen

Die Auswanderung erfolgte gewöhnlich in drei Etappen: Zunächst musste der Weg vom Heimatort zum nächstgelegenen Hafen bewältigt werden. Dort traten die Auswanderer die Überfahrt nach Amerika per Schiff an. Der letzte Teil der Reise führte dann ins Landesinnere an den Zielort in der neuen Heimat.

In der ersten Hälfte des 19. Jahrhunderts mussten die Auswanderungswilligen bis nach Le Havre (Frankreich), Rotterdam (Holland) oder Liverpool (England) fahren, um ihr Schiff zu erreichen. Sie gingen zu Fuß, fuhren auf Wagen oder in der Kutsche und schließlich weiter auf Flussschiffen (Rhein, Main, Weser) an die Küste. Erst mit dem Ausbau des Eisenbahnnetzes ab 1850 wurden die deutschen Überseehäfen Bremen (Bremerhaven) und Hamburg auch für die Auswanderer aus Bayern schnell erreichbar.

‹ zurück weiter ›

In den Hafenstädten mussten die Auswanderer manchmal wochenlang auf das Auslaufen ihres Segelschiffs warten. Hier kauften sie die vorgeschriebene Ausrüstung und zusätzliche Verpflegung für die Überfahrt. Um die Ortsfremden vor Geschäftemachern zu schützen und gleichzeitig den guten Ruf der Stadt als Auswandererhafen zu wahren, richtete der Bremer Magistrat bereits um 1845 eine „Inspektion für das Auswanderungswesen" ein. Sie wachte darüber, dass die Auswanderer nicht übervorteilt wurden. Hamburg folgte dem Bremer Vorbild mit einer ähnlichen Behörde. Zur Unterbringung der durchreisenden Menschenmenge wurden in beiden Städten eigene „Auswandererhallen" gebaut, wo die Wartenden eine Unterkunft fanden.

Überfahrt

Der Fortschritt im Schiffsbau veränderte innerhalb weniger Jahrzehnte die Überfahrt für die Auswanderer grundlegend. In der ersten Hälfte des 19. Jahrhunderts hatte man nur behelfsmäßig auf die plötzlich ansteigende Nachfrage nach Passagierplätzen reagiert. In die Frachtschiffe wurde ein Zwischendeck eingezogen, in dem fortan die Masse der Auswanderer auf engstem Raum und ohne hinreichende Belüftung befördert wurde. Die schlechten hygienischen Verhältnisse und die oft ungenügende Verpflegung kosteten vielen Auswanderern das Leben.

Mit dem Einsatz der neuen geräumigen Dampfschiffe verkürzte sich die Fahrzeit eines Seglers von bisher acht bis 12 Wochen auf wenige Tage. Die erste regelmäßige transatlantische Verbindung wurde am 8. April 1838 vom britischen Dampfer „Great Western" eröffnet: Er benötigte für die Strecke von Bristol nach New York nur mehr 15 Tage und 5 Stunden. Da die Fahrt auf Dampfschiffen aber sehr kostspielig war, nutzten die Auswanderer bis zur Mitte des Jahrhunderts weiterhin überwiegend Segelschiffe. 1870 waren allerdings bereits 88 Prozent aller Schiffe Dampfer. Durch das rasch wachsende Angebot an Überfahrtsplätzen verringerte sich bald auch der Preis. Die Fahrt nach Amerika war also nicht mehr so beschwerlich. Doch auch im Zeitalter der Ozeanriesen blieb die Atlantiküberquerung gefährlich, wie der Untergang der „Titanic" im April 1912 zeigt.

Quelle: Reinhold Albert, Auswanderung aus Sulzdorf und Umgebung nach Amerika von 1835–1900, http://www.sulzdorf.rhoen-saale.net/fileServer/LKRG/1031/13439/PDF_-_AuswanderungAmerika-2.pdf

Step up!

Häufig wirst du nicht alle deutschen **Wörter** im Englischen kennen. Du musst diese aber nicht unbedingt im Wörterbuch nachschlagen, sondern kannst diese **umschreiben** oder **erklären**. Hilfreich sind dabei z. B.

- Relativsätze (Pferdekutsche → *a coach which is drawn by horses*)
- die Verwendung von Verben statt Nomen (Belüftung → *to get fresh air into a room*)
- die Trennung zusammengesetzter Nomen (das Landesinnere → *the heart/centre of a country*) ■

c) Here are some difficult words and phrases from the German text. Try to explain what they mean in English. There is one example.

der Ausbau des Eisenbahnnetzes	*railway connections were improved/became better/ there were more and more trains*
Flussschiff	
Überseehafen	
Verpflegung	
das rasch wachsende Angebot an Überfahrtsplätzen	

d) Write an e-mail to Tom in return in which you provide all the information asked for. The start and end of the email have already been written for you.

Step up!
Beachte, dass bereits Teile der E-Mail vorgegeben sind und du diesen informellen **Stil** fortführen musst. ■

New Message

To tommyy@yummy.com

Subject RE: Immigration to US

Hi Tom

Good to hear from you. I hope you enjoyed your vacation.
It's funny, we're talking about immigration to the US in our English class, too.
So let's see if I can help you.

Hope that helps!
Yours
Finn

Send

Step up!
Überprüfe deine Texte abschließend immer noch einmal auf **Vollständigkeit** und **sprachliche Richtigkeit**. Achte auch darauf, dass sie wirklich **nur relevante Informationen** enthalten und dass die **Sprache** zu Zieltext und Adressaten passt. ■

Topic 30: Strategien zur Sprachmittlung

92 In diesem Kapitel hast du verschiedene Strategien verwendet, um Texte vom Deutschen ins Englische zu mitteln und umgekehrt. Suche die Strategien (in den Topics und Aufgaben des Kapitels) und trage sie in der folgenden Tabelle ein. Du musst entscheiden, ob es sich um eine *pre-*, *while-* oder *post-mediation* Strategie handelt.

Mediation Strategies
Vor der Sprachmittlung: ➡ ➡ ➡ ➡ ➡ Bei Hörtexten ... ➡ Welcher Zieltext soll erstellt werden (z. B. E-Mail, Vortrag); was sind typische Merkmale dieser Textsorte?
Während der Sprachmittlung: ➡ Was muss ggf. ergänzt werden? – zusätzliche Informationen bei sehr kurzen Texten (S. 84) – – ➡ ➡ Wörter im Wörterbuch nachschlagen (S. 92, 96) ➡ ➡
Nach der Sprachmittlung: ➡ Schriftliche Zieltexte nochmals in Hinblick auf die Überlegungen, die du im Vorfeld angestellt hast, überprüfen (S. 103) ➡

Writing –
Wie du deine Schreibkompetenz verbessern kannst

Beim Schreiben zusammenhängender Texte musst du dich je nach **Textsorte** darauf konzentrieren, neugierig zu machen, interessante Themen zu erörtern, Spannung zu erzeugen, fesselnd zu beschreiben oder wichtige Informationen zu vermitteln. Leser*innen verlieren ansonsten die Lust, weiterzulesen, oder beginnen erst gar nicht zu lesen.

- Daher ist es ratsam, nicht einfach „draufloszuschreiben“ und gedanklich hin und her zu springen, denn das erschwert es ungemein, den Inhalt deines Textes zu verstehen.
- Stattdessen solltest du deine Gedanken und Ideen vorab ordnen und sie dann in einzelnen, klar strukturierten **Abschnitten** darbieten. Auf diese Weise kann man deinem Gedankengang besser folgen.
- Beim Schreiben der Abschnitte solltest du beachten, dass die verschiedenen **Textsorten** in der Regel einem besonderen **Aufbau** folgen. Dieser erleichtert das Verständnis und sollte daher eingehalten werden. In den *Step up!*-Kästen wird dir dieser Aufbau detailliert erläutert.
- Die folgenden *Topics* beschäftigen sich mit den verschiedenen Textformen, die in der achten Klasse von Bedeutung sind (Brief/E-Mail, Tagebucheintrag, Textzusammenfassung und argumentativer Text). Wie in den übrigen Kapiteln werden dir auch **Strategien** zur Verbesserung deiner Schreibkompetenz aufgezeigt.
- Erstelle dir mithilfe der Tabelle am Ende des Kapitels eine **Übersicht** über alle Strategien, die du vor, während oder nach dem Schreiben anwenden kannst. Du kannst diese in Zukunft immer zur Hilfe nehmen, wenn du einen Text schreibst.

Topic 31: A day in NYC

93 Imagine that you are an exchange student attending a US high school and living with a host family. At the moment you are on a sightseeing trip to New York City for two days. Back at the youth hostel at the end of the first day, you want to write an email to your host family. Considering the situation and whom you are writing to, what should this email be like? Tick (✓) the most probable answers. Sometimes there is more than one solution.

a) Your email should be …
- ☐ very short.
- ☐ nice and friendly.
- ☐ polite.
- ☐ funny.

b) What should you write about?
- ☐ You should give information about your trip and your experiences.
- ☐ You have to give them historical information about New York.
- ☐ Your description should be positive rather than negative because you do not want your host parents to worry about you.
- ☐ You can complain about everything that you did not like there.

c) What language should you use?
- ☐ You write in German.
- ☐ You write in formal English.
- ☐ You write in informal English.

Step up!

Vorüberlegungen beim Verfassen einer E-Mail bzw. eines Briefs
- Versetze dich immer in die **vorgegebene Situation** und vergegenwärtige dir stets, wer der **Adressat** des Textes ist.
- Je nachdem, an wen sich dein Schreiben richtet, wirst du eine eher **persönliche oder eher formelle Sprache** wählen. In einem Schreiben an Gleichaltrige wirst du anders schreiben, als wenn du dich an Erwachsene wendest. In einem Brief an jemanden, den du nicht kennst, wirst du höflicher und förmlicher schreiben, als wenn du dich an einen Freund wendest. ■

94 Now you need some facts about your trip to New York. Fill in the following grid and invent some information about …

- when and how you arrived.
- who else you travelled with.
- how you like the youth hostel.
- where you have been, and when, what means of transportation you used to get there, what you saw/visited (sightseeing tour) and what it was like.

Step up!

Planung eines Textes

Bevor du beginnst, einen Text zu verfassen, solltest du dir Gedanken zum Inhalt machen. Um deine Ideen zu sammeln, kannst du z. B:

- eine **Mindmap** erstellen, um dir Zusammenhänge vor Augen zu führen.
- eine **Tabelle** anlegen, in der du die wichtigsten Informationen sammelst und strukturierst.
- die **W-Fragen** beantworten: „wer" *(who)*, „was" *(what)*, „wann" *(when)*, „wo" *(where)* und nicht zu vergessen „wie" *(how)*. ■

These pictures may help you with your story.

- Where: New York
- Why: Sightseeing
- Who: ____________

Step up!

Über Erlebnisse schreiben
Wenn du Eindrücke und Erlebnisse beschreiben sollst, brauchst du **ausdrucksstarke Adjektive**, wie z. B. *absolutely awesome, truly amazing, fantastic, actually pretty cool, marvellous, just breathtaking, pretty impressive, extremely exciting.* ■

Sightseeing trip that day		
When	**Where / What**	**What it was like**
8 a.m.	arrival by bus at ferry terminal in Manhattan; you could see the Statue of Liberty	awesome and breathtaking to see the Statue of Liberty
after arrival	Statue of Liberty, climbed steps up to the crown	
evening	arrival at the youth hostel	

95 In order to help you with your e-mail, a friend of yours lets you read the e-mail he wrote to his host mother from his trip to L.A. Mark any expressions which you could use for your email.

New Message

To: cat@morgan.com Cc Bcc

Subject: Greetings from L.A.

Dear Cathy
L.A. is just absolutely awesome! Chloe and I had such a fantastic day today! After a long night on the bus, we arrived in Hollywood early in the morning. The first thing we went to was the Walk of Fame! That was truly amazing! It suddenly hit home that we really are in Los Angeles!
Totally thrilled, we booked a Movie Stars' Homes Tour on a minibus. Now, you probably think, "Oh no, seeing the homes of celebrities hidden behind huge fences, that must be boring!", but our tour guide was actually great fun and gave us lots of information on how the rich and the famous live. We also drove past some important sights, such as the Hollywood Sign. It was quite an experience being there!
After a few hours the bus took us to a restaurant which sold chicken and waffles. The food was delicious. After that, we walked through the streets and did some shopping.
In the afternoon we took a bus to Santa Monica Pier, which took forever, but it paid off, as the sun was setting when we reached the beach!
On our way to the hostel we stopped at an Italian deli and bakery and had a yummy sandwich for dinner.
When we finally made it home to our youth hostel, I was so excited that I didn't care that the youth hostel was quite rundown. Chloe was a little shocked. My room, however, is clean, so don't worry!
See you soon
Koray

Send

96 a) Use your grid and the structure and expressions from Koray's text to write an email to your host family about your trip to New York City.
Write about 250–300 words.

Step up!

Aufbau einer E-Mail/eines Briefes

introduction → Die Einleitung beinhaltet eine allgemeine Aussage darüber wie es dir geht und/oder über das Thema deines Schreibens.

main part → Der Hauptteil beschreibt z. B.
- die wichtigsten Fakten und Informationen an den Adressaten,
- Beschreibungen und Erzählungen,
- deine persönlichen Ansichten und Meinungen.

conclusion → Der Schluss beinhaltet z. B.
- einen Satz über die momentane Situation, in der man sich befindet,
- welche Pläne es für die Zukunft gibt,
- eine Aufforderung/Bitte an den Adressaten. ■

b) Proofread your email and correct any mistake you find.

Step up!

Achte bei der Korrektur deiner Texte auf
- die konsequente Verwendung der richtigen **Sprachform** (*formal/informal English*), z. B. *short forms.*
- die Gliederung des Textes durch **Absätze**.
- die Anwendung der richtigen **Zeitformen** (*tenses*).
- den Gebrauch möglichst vieler *connectives* (z. B. *anyway, but, so, then* etc.), um zeitliche **Abfolgen** und logische **Zusammenhänge** deutlich zu machen. ■

97 In his email Koray mentions that the youth hostel was not very good. His friend Chloe actually had a horrible night there. After the trip, she writes a letter of complaint to the manager.

Use her notes and the Step up!-boxes below to write her formal letter.

dirty
- hair of previous guest all over the bathroom
- trash on the floor
- dirty bedlinen ("Bettwäsche"): stains ("Flecken")

address:
LA Youth Hostel
1212 Ocean Blvd
Los Angeles
CA 90028

one night
18–19 May

costs:
$64 for one single room for one night
=> I want a refund ("Rückerstattung")

- person at the reception promised to have the room cleaned
=> nobody came to do the cleaning

Step up!

Sprache in geschäftlichen E-Mails/Briefen
Wenn du einer Firma, Institution oder (relativ) fremden Person eine E-Mail/einen Brief schreibst, verwendest du:
- ***formal English*, d.h.**
  - Schriftsprache,
  - *long forms*, z. B. *does not, cannot, would, would not* etc.,
- **formale Grußformeln**
  Wenn du den Namen des Empfängers **kennst**:
  - **Anrede**: Dear Mr …/ Dear Ms …/ Dear Mrs …
  - **Schlussformel**: Yours sincerely …/US: Sincerely (yours) …

  Wenn du den Namen des Empfängers **nicht kennst**:
  - **Anrede**: Dear Sir / Dear Madam / Dear Sir or Madam
  - **Schlussformel**: Yours faithfully …/US: Sincerely (yours) … ■

Chloe Hamilton
7740 West Academy Avenue
Lakewood, CO 80226

LA Youth Hostel
…
…

May …

Re:

Yours …

Chloe Hamilton

Chloe Hamilton

Step up!

Aufbau eines geschäftlichen Briefes

sender	→	Name und Adresse des Absenders
addressee	→	Name und Adresse des Empfängers
date	→	Achte auf die richtige Schreibweise des Datums, z.B. 15 June 20 .. (BE), May 16, 20 .. (AE)
Re	→	Stichwort(e) zum Thema/ Inhalt des Briefes ■

98 After your year as an exchange student at a US high school, you are back home in Germany. Write an e-mail to your American host family to let them know
- that you had a safe journey home,
- why this year was special to you and
- what you want to thank them for.

Step up!

Sprache in informellen E-Mails/Briefen
Wenn du deiner Familie, Freunden oder Bekannten eine E-Mail/ einen Brief schreibst, verwendest du:

- ***informal English*, d.h.**
  - eher Ausdrücke der Umgangssprache,
  - *short forms*, z. B. *doesn't, can't, I'd, wouldn't* etc.,
- **umgangssprachliche Grußformeln, wie**
  - **Anrede**: Dear .../ Hi ..../ Hello ...
  - **Schlussformel**: Best wishes .../ All the best .../ Take care .../ Love .../ Yours ... ■

Topic 32: Celebrating Thanksgiving in the US

99 a) You are an exchange student living with a host family in the USA. At high school, you learned what the holiday of Thanksgiving is about. Here are your notes. Read them carefully.

Thanksgiving

is a very important holiday in the United States, celebrated on the fourth Thursday in November.

History: what is known as the "First Thanksgiving" was celebrated in 1621 by the Pilgrims, the first large group of settlers in North America; they wanted to thank God for their first harvest *(Ernte)* in America

Celebration: traditionally, US families meet and have a Thanksgiving dinner; they usually eat turkey, mashed potatoes *(Kartoffelbrei)* and vegetables

- they often pray before and after the meal, thanking God for all the good things that happened to them during the year
- in some towns there are parades
- American football or other sports are an important part of Thanksgiving celebrations in the USA; there are always important games on TV and in the local stadiums *(Stadion)*

b) You want to write your travel diary and talk about Thanksgiving celebration with your host family. Start off by making a mind map. Take notes on …
- **who** was there,
- **what** you did, **where** you were and **how** it was,
- **what** kind of food you had and **how** you liked it,
- **what** you liked best about your host family's Thanksgiving celebration and **why**.

You may use the photo and the notes about Thanksgiving.

Step up!

Verfassen eines Tagebucheintrags

In einem *diary entry* schreibt eine Person über ihre Erlebnisse, ihre Probleme, ihre Gefühle, ihre Hoffnungen, Sorgen und Pläne.
- Nimm stets die **Perspektive** der von dir gewählten Person ein.
- Die gewählten Eigenschaften sowie die **Gedanken** und **Gefühle** deiner Person müssen zueinander passen. ■

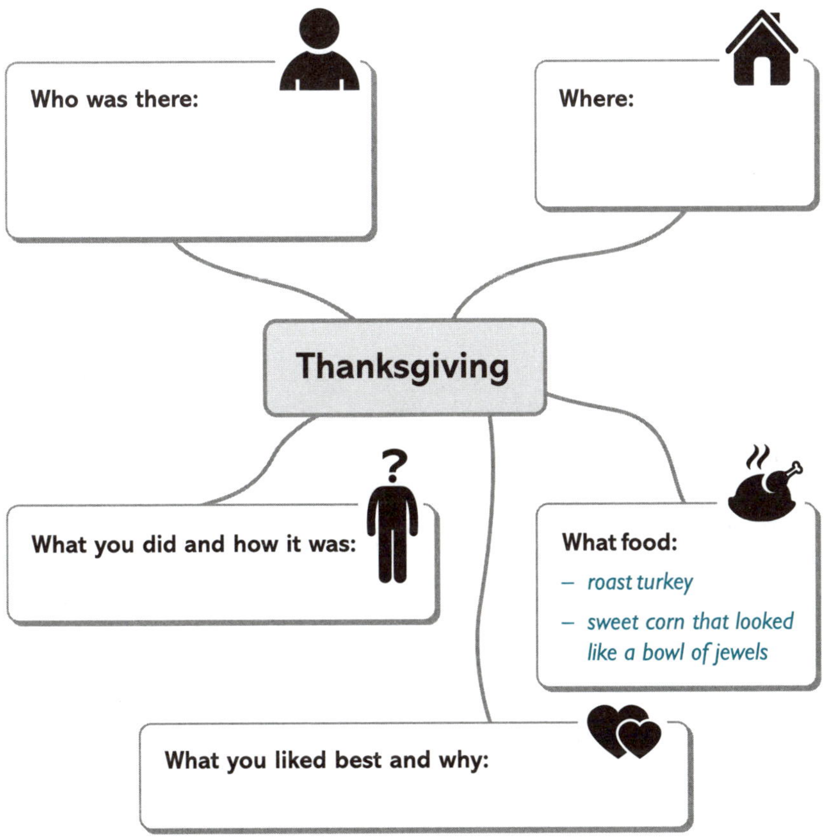

Step up!

Erlebnisse genau beschreiben

Möchte man ein Ereignis **möglichst genau und detailliert** beschreiben, spielen Gefühle und Sinneseindrücke eine wichtige Rolle:

- Die fünf Sinne (**Sehen**, **Schmecken**, **Fühlen**, **Riechen**, **Hören**) sollten möglichst oft angesprochen werden.
- Verwende **ausdrucksstarke Adjektive**, um genau zu beschreiben und zu bewerten. ■

100 Now, check your ideas in the mind map. Where can you address one or more senses? Highlight existing notes or add ideas. Use a different coloured pen for each of the five senses seeing, tasting, feeling, smelling and hearing.

101 Use the ideas in your mind map to write a diary entry of how you celebrated Thanksgiving with your host family. Remember to structure your text correctly. Write 250–300 words.

Step up!

Aufbau eines Tagebucheintrags

Date	z. B.: "4 November 20 . . "
Opening formula	z. B.: "Dear Diary"
Introduction	Die **Einleitung** beinhaltet eine allgemeine Aussage über den Tag oder den Gemütszustand des Verfassers/der Verfasserin.
Main part	Der **Hauptteil** beschreibt, • was eine Person erlebt hat, • wie sie sich dabei gefühlt hat und • welche Hoffnungen, Sorgen und/oder Pläne sie für die Zukunft hegt.
Conclusion	Der **Schluss** beinhaltet eine abschließende Aussage über den Tag oder die Gefühle der Person oder einen Satz über die momentane Situation, in der sich die Person befindet. ■

102 The next important holiday, Christmas, is over. Write a diary entry of how you celebrated Christmas with your US host family.

Topic 33: To catch a thief

103 When you write a summary, you have to follow certain rules about form and content.

a) Look at the following aspects and decide what belongs in the first sentence of your summary.

- ☐ author
- ☐ title
- ☐ length of the text
- ☐ form of text, e.g. newspaper article, (short) story, poem
- ☐ date/year of publication
- ☐ place of publication
- ☐ short description of what the text is about (who? what? where? when?)
- ☐ personal opinion on the text

b) In a summary, which of the following are do's and which are don'ts?

	do	don't
❶ use your own words	☐	☐
❷ use quotes from the text/direct speech	☐	☐
❸ use mostly present tenses	☐	☐
❹ use the first person (e.g. "I think")	☐	☐
❺ use short forms (e.g. "hasn't", "won't")	☐	☐
❻ include details on the persons in the text	☐	☐

104 a) Read the text. Some of the new words are given below.

b) Then describe what the text is about by asking yourself **the questions below**. You will need this information for your introductory paragraph.

- Who: ______________________
- What: ______________________

  ____
- Where: ______________________
- When: ______________________

Text To catch a thief

He very carefully felt for the screwdriver[1] and the razor blade[2] in the right-hand pocket of his jacket. I hope I don't cut myself with it right in the middle of the job. That would be rather nasty[3]. The blood would stain the 501 jeans and very soon everybody could tell ... The screwdriver was no problem, but it had not been too easy to get hold of a razor blade in his house. His father and his older brother Dwane preferred electric razors. They both hated shaving foam[4] and blades. Perhaps his mother would keep razor blades in her sewing basket[5], but he hadn't dared to ask her. She would have wanted to know what on earth he needed a razor blade for. Luckily he remembered that his little sister Charmaine had asked for a razor blade some days ago. She had said she needed it for something they did in their arts lessons. And sure enough, on going through her arts utensils he had found the blade. He just hoped he would hold it the right way round to cut the tag[6] off the jeans!

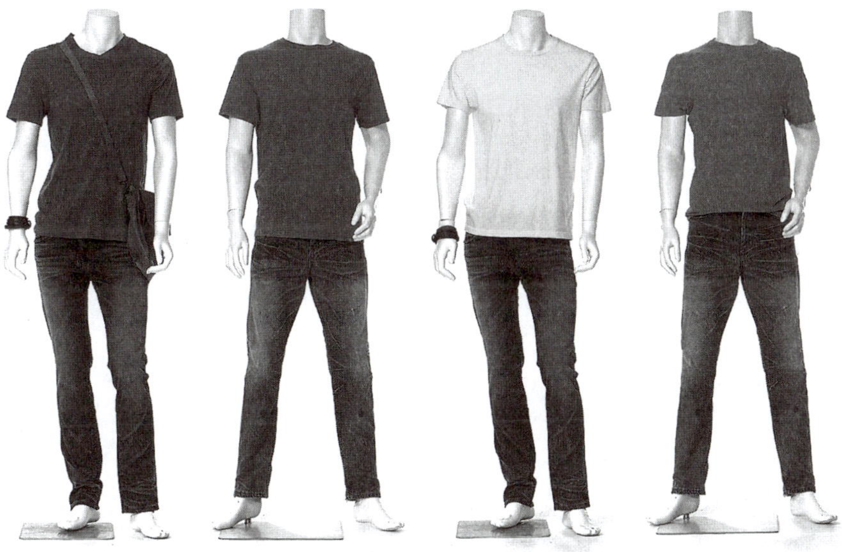

He was glad that the store was so busy. Parents were trying to do their shopping and keep an eye on their kids at the same time. A few kids were running around and screaming, playing hide and seek[7]. Mothers were shouting. Shop assistants hated this time of the week, most of them looked tired and were probably looking forward to closing time. But 6 o'clock was still more than two hours away! He knew he had enough time.

There were not so many customers in the men's department. He went to the section with exquisite clothing, browsed around[8] and finally picked the most expensive jeans in his size. You were allowed to take three items at a time into the changing room to try on. That would be convenient[9]. Inside the cubicle[10] he carefully took out the screwdriver and the razor blade and began to remove the tag. Don't cut into the fine cloth, he said to himself. Relax. Easy, you have all the time in the world. It was hard going, but eventually the tag came off. He put on the new jeans, and then his old ones over the top. Wearing two pairs of jeans at the same time seemed a bit uncomfortable at first, but he knew he would be alright and make it home. He picked up the other two pairs, pulled the curtain aside and placed those jeans back on the rack. Lots of people were trying on Levi's in various sizes and colours. He heard one mother saying, "I'm not going to pay that much just for a pair of jeans. Why don't you take one from the 'reduced' rack, Kevin?" "But Mum, they aren't fashionable! None of the kids in my class wear those!" the youngster complained. What a good job his mother wasn't here! He turned round and headed for the escalator to take him down to the first floor and the main entrance. He passed the electronic theft-protection gate without any trouble. He smiled to himself, rather pleased. "Excuse me, young man." Turning round he saw a grey-haired, middle-aged man with glasses. "I am the store detective. Would you follow me to my office, please."

Jacob, Rainer: To catch a thief. In: Abenteuergeschichten. Hallbergmoos: Stark Verlag (1997).

Annotations

1 screwdriver: *Schraubenzieher*
2 razor blade: *Rasierklinge*
3 nasty: *scheußlich, grässlich, widerlich*
4 shaving foam: *Rasierschaum*
5 sewing basket: *Nähkasten*
6 tag: *Etikett; hier: Diebstahlschutz*
7 (to) play hide and seek: *Verstecken spielen*
8 (to) browse around: *sich umsehen, stöbern*
9 convenient: *praktisch, günstig, bequem*
10 cubicle: *Kabine*

105 Divide the text into different passages and write down keywords/-phrases. Then find headlines for each passage using your own words as much as possible.

Passage	Keywords/-phrases	Headline
ll. 1–4		

Step up!

Einleitungssatz

Der Einleitungssatz beinhaltet folgende Informationen:

- **Autor, Titel, Textform, Veröffentlichungsjahr**
- worum es in dem Text geht (**wer?, was?** und falls wichtig auch **wo?, wann?**)

Gute Anfänge sind:

- *The* **Textform "Titel"** *written by* **Autor** *and published in* **Erscheinungsjahr** *is about …* **(wer?, was?, ggf. wo?, wann?)**
- *The* **Textform "Titel"** (**Erscheinungsjahr**) *written by* **Autor** *is about …* **(wer?, was?, wo?, wann?)** ■

106 Before you write your summary, look at what Aiden wrote.

a) He made quite a few mistakes in his introductory sentence. Can you correct them?

> The short story "A Thief" written of Rainer Jacob and in 1997 is on a man who steals a pair of jeans.

b) Aiden also wrote some notes on the information he wants to include in the text, but he goes into too much detail. Cross out the information which is not important for the summary.

> - A teenage boy carries a screwdriver and a razor.
> - He is worried that he will hurt himself when using the razor.
> - finding a screwdriver at home = easy
> - finding a razor = very hard
> - His older brother Dwane and his father like electric razors.
> - He has been afraid to ask his mum whether she has any razors because she might ask questions.
> - He has taken the razor from his sister's arts class material.
> - The young man is happy that he picked the right time for shoplifting: about 3:30 pm.

- The shop assistants won't pay much attention to him.
- They are weary: they have already been working for hours.
- They have a lot to do because the shop is full of families.
- lots of time to get everything done
- Everything goes according to plan.
- He picks the jeans that cost the most and two more pairs of jeans to throw on the rack later on.
- goes to a cubicle
- Inside the changing room, he uses the screwdriver and the razor to get the tag off. "Don't cut into the fine cloth," he told himself.
- Wearing the stolen jeans under his old jeans he goes down towards the exit and passes the electronic theft-protection gate successfully.
- At that moment, right before leaving the shop, the store detective stops the thief and takes the young man to his office.

107 Write your summary.

Step up!

Eine Zusammenfassung schreiben

- Schreibe die Zusammenfassung mit deinen **eigenen Worten** und übernehme nur die Wörter aus dem Text, zu denen du keine Alternative kennst.
- Schreibe die Zusammenfassung im ***simple present*** und ***present perfect***. (Für Ereignisse, die vor der Handlung im Text oder nach dieser stattfinden, musst du das *simple past* bzw. das *will future* verwenden.)
- Verwende **Konjunktionen** (z .B. *and, but, so, before, after, so, since, when, then, later*).
- Verwende niemals direkte Rede und Textzitate. Gehe nicht zu sehr ins Detail.
- Die Einleitung bildet einen eigenen Absatz. Der Rest der Zusammenfassung hat in der Regel keine weitere Untergliederung in Absätze. ■

Topic 34: Tornado in Iowa

108 For a writing competition with the topic "Dangerous nature" you want to write a story about a tornado. To do that, you first did some research on the internet. These are your notes:

Tornado

- *It is a rotating[1] column[2] of air which touches the earth and a large, dark cloud above.*
- *It carries dust and debris[3].*
- *A tornado might be coming when there is:*
  - → *a dark sky,*
  - → *a large, dark cloud,*
  - → *lots of wind,*
  - → *hail[4]*
  - → *and a loud noise that sounds like a train.*
- *A tornado can come suddenly without warning, but often people have about 10 minutes between the tornado warning and its arrival.*
- *Safety rules:*
  - → *at home*
    - *seek shelter[5] in a storm cellar[6] (many homes in the Midwest of the USA have one) or*
    - *seek shelter in the middle of the basement, far away from windows, because an exploding window can injure or kill (e.g. the hallway, the bathroom, the closet).*
    - *get under something (e.g. a heavy table) to protect you from falling debris.*
    - *cover your body with a blanket or anything available.*
    - *get on your knees with your elbows on the ground, covering your head with your arms.*
  - → *on the road/outside*
    - *leave your car, bus etc., as they can easily be caught up by a tornado.*
    - *do not go under a bridge – the wind speed can be worse there.*
    - *find a place far away from any trees and lie down on the ground, covering your head with your arms.*

Annotations

1 rotating: *rotierend, sich drehend*
2 column: *Säule*
3 debris: *Trümmer, Schutt*
4 hail: *Hagel*
5 seek shelter: *Schutz suchen*
6 storm cellar: *Sturmschutzraum*

For the setting of your story, look at the picture below. It shows a small part of the American town Woodward, Iowa after a tornado had hit it on the afternoon of Saturday, 12 November 2005.

Write down details of the setting as shown in the picture. Some of the words and expressions used in the notes above might be useful here.

109 The general topic of your story is clear: a tornado hits some parts of Woodward.

- What happens in your story exactly?
- Who is/are your main character/s? What is/are the main character/s like? Make sure your character/s is/are realistic and your plot is interesting!

Step up!

Vorüberlegungen beim Verfassen einer „Story“

- Wo und wann trägt sich deine Geschichte zu? → *„setting“*
- Was passiert in deiner Geschichte (in welcher Reihenfolge)? → *„plot“*
- Wer ist/sind die handelnde/n Person/en? → *„characters“*
- Welche Stimmung hat deine Geschichte? → *„mood/atmosphere“*
- Wer erzählt die Geschichte (aus welcher Perspektive)? → *„narrator“ (point of view)* ■

Fill in the mind map below. If necessary, make use of a dictionary to look up words and expressions.

PLOT

What happens first, next, after that?

MAIN CHARACTER

Male? Female?

Age

What is he/she like?

What relationship do they have?

- husband and wife?
- mother and child?
- …

ANOTHER MAIN CHARACTER (optional)

Male? Female?

Age

What is he/she like?

110 Read the information in the Step up!-box carefully.

Decide which of the following ideas about a plot would be part of the *exposition, rising action, climax* and *falling action* of the story. Note them down in the grid.

❶ The tornado is moving towards the house.

❷ The main characters leave the house. Luckily, they are not injured.

❸ The main characters hear a tornado warning.

❹ The roof of the house is destroyed.

Exposition	
Rising action	
Climax	
Falling action	

Step up!

Aufbau einer Geschichte

Exposition Die Exposition stellt der Leserschaft
- Ort,
- Zeit und
- Hauptperson(en) vor und
- benennt ggf. eine vorangegangene Situation.

Rising action Dieser Teil der Geschichte
- beschreibt eine besondere Situation/Schlüsselsituation, in der die Hauptperson(en) sich befindet/befinden und
- baut dabei zunehmend Spannung auf.

Climax Der Höhepunkt ist der Teil der *story*, in dem die Situation, mit der die Hauptperson(en) konfrontiert ist/sind, besonders dramatisch ist/gelöst wird.
Dieser höchste Punkt der Handlung ist häufig ein Wendepunkt *(turning point)*. Danach nimmt die Spannung ab.

Falling action Im anschließenden, letzten Teil der Geschichte
- wird geschildert, wie es für die Hauptperson(en) nach der besonderen Situation, in der sie sich befunden hat/haben, weitergeht.
- Dabei nimmt die Spannung stark ab. ■

111 Every story has a certain atmosphere, which can also change during the story. Look at your plot ideas. Then add adjectives/adverbs and further details that will create the atmosphere you want in each part of your story.

Step up!

Die Stimmung einer Geschichte

Die Stimmung einer Geschichte wird durch die Art, in der man die Handlung, die Figuren und den Ort des Geschehens beschreibt, beeinflusst. Hierzu verwendet man passende

- Adjektive und Adverbien sowie
- (Neben-)Sätze, die die Figuren und das Setting näher beschreiben.

For example: The tornado came closer.

The huge tornado came closer with unbelievable force. We started to scream wildly.

	Plot	Atmosphere	
		adjectives/ adverbs	description of details
Exposition			
Rising action		large, dark (cloud)	
Climax			
Falling action			

112 Decide who tells the reader the story. Tick the box and read the examples so you know what to watch out for.

✓	**Erzähler**	**Beispiel**
	first-person narrator (a character in the story)	"Yesterday, **I** had just made **myself** a cup of coffee in **my** home in Woodward, Iowa, when …"
	third-person narrator (outside the story)	"Yesterday, **Susan** had just made **herself** a cup of coffee in **her** home …"

113 Write your interesting, exciting story for the competition. Write about 300 words. Decide on a catchy title once you have finished your story.

Step up!

Überschrift
Den Titel solltest du deiner Geschichte nach Fertigstellung geben, damit er

- gut zu der gesamten Geschichte passt und
- Interesse weckt, ohne zu viel zu verraten. ■

114 Read the model story in the key and write a story from the perspective of Susan's parents.

Thinking about these questions might help:

- Did they get the tornado warning?
- Did they see the tornado?
- Were they safe?
- Did the tornado hit their home or were they lucky?
- Arriving at Susan's house to check if she was safe, what did they find?

Topic 35: "Cliques are good for teenagers!"

115 Look at the following pictures. Which clique would you want to belong to and why?

I would like to belong to clique ☐ because ______________________

____

____

Clique ☐ is a group I would not want to belong to because ______________

____

____

Step up!

Kommentar

Beim Verfassen eines Kommentars musst du
- deine Meinung klar und deutlich zum Ausdruck bringen,
- starke Argumente, Begründungen und Beispiele sammeln, um die Leserschaft von deiner Meinung zu überzeugen. ■

116 a) Ask yourself what benefits (+) and what dangers (–) cliques can have. Add your arguments to the table below.

Statement: “Cliques are good/dangerous for teenagers”	
+ (advantages)	**– (disadvantages)**
Your opinion:	

b) Look at the benefits and dangers you have noted down. Then decide what your opinion is on the statement “Cliques are good for teenagers!” Add it to the table.

Step up!

Argumente

- Üblicherweise beginnt man für jedes **Argument** einen neuen **Absatz**.
- Das heißt, jeder **Absatz** behandelt lediglich **einen Aspekt**, der im ersten Satz – dem sogenannten ***topic sentence*** – eingeleitet wird.
- Die übrigen Sätze untermauern das jeweilige Argument mit zusätzlichen **Details**, **Erklärungen** oder **Beispielen**. Man nennt sie daher ***supporting sentences***. ■

117 Read the example paragraph and underline its topic sentence. Then look at the supporting sentences and highlight any definitions, explanations or examples you find.

Example argument:

Cliques are groups of people that share interests and exclude people who are different. In every school there are different cliques because there is a great number of different things that people can have in common. For example, loving the same kind of music, being a fan of the same sport, etc. can be the reason why teenagers are in a clique together. Teenagers who are not part of these groups are left out.

118 Read the supporting sentences below. Then tick the best topic sentence for them.

Topic sentence 1	**A clique weakens a teenager's self-confidence.**	☐
Topic sentence 2	**A clique makes a teenager more confident.**	☐
Topic sentence 3	**There are reasons why teenagers often feel insecure[1].**	☐
Topic sentence 4	**Teenagers join a clique to no longer feel alone.**	☐
supporting sentences	Teenagers are on their way from being children to becoming adults. Their bodies and minds change. Because of that, some young people feel insecure. Often, they think that, adults like their parents do not understand them, so they join a clique to have a place where they fit in and belong. Here they have friends that have the same interests. As a result, they feel understood and accepted and their self-confidence grows.	

Annotation

1 insecure: unsicher

119 a) Read the topic sentence and the notes for supporting sentences below. Turn the notes into complete sentences.

topic sentence	Being part of a clique, teenagers always have people that are there for them through life's ups and downs.
supporting sentences – notes	other teenagers • be mean to • a member of a clique • clique • help you bad grades at school • study with you advice • problems something wonderful happens • clique • listen • happy for you great • part of a clique
supporting sentences	

b) Use some of the "useful phrases" from the box below to improve the style of your paragraph.

Step up!

Nützliche Wendungen (*connecting phrases*)

- … zur Strukturierung: *first / second / third …* • *on the one hand … / on the other hand …* • *more or less* • *furthermore* • *finally*
- … zum Zusammenhang: *because (of that)* • *although* • *however* • *in spite of* • *in order to* • *in fact* • *so* • *as a result* • *for example* • *(even) more importantly* • *at the same time* ■

120 Now choose two to four arguments you want to use and number them in the table in task 116 to show in what order you want to use them. Read the information in the Step up!-box before you start.

Step up!

Die Reihenfolge der Argumente

Der Hauptteil des Kommentars bringt 2 bis 4 überzeugende Argumente, die die eigene Meinung untermauern.

<u>Wenn man klar dafür oder dagegen ist,</u>

- beginnt man mit einem wichtigen, starken Argument, das die eigene Meinung untermauert, um die Aufmerksamkeit der Leserschaft zu erlangen und
- endet mit dem allerwichtigsten und stärksten Argument, da dies den Leserinnen und Lesern am besten in Erinnerung bleibt.
- Ggf. behandelt man ein bis maximal zwei nicht so starke Argumente dazwischen.

<u>Wenn man sowohl Argumente dafür als auch dagegen hat, aber zu einer Seite tendiert,</u>

- beginnt man mit 1–2 Gegenargumenten.
- Erst danach behandelt man 2 (max. 3) Argumente, die die eigene Meinung untermauern. Auch hier steht das stärkste Argument am Schluss. Dadurch kann man die Leserinnen und Leser stärker beeinflussen. ■

Step up!

Aufbau einer Einleitung

Die **Einleitung *(introduction)*** stellt das Thema vor und soll den Leser auf den Text einstimmen und/oder Interesse wecken. Du hast eine der folgenden Möglichkeiten:

- Nenne das ***statement*** bzw. das Thema.
  Beispiel: *Cliques are good for teenagers.*
- Weise auf die **Bedeutung** des Themas hin.
  Beispiel: *Almost every teenager is part of a clique.*
- Zeige **unterschiedliche Meinungen** zum Thema auf.
  Beispiel: *Psychologists and many pupils think cliques are good for teenagers. Parents often disagree.*
- Stelle **deine Meinung** vor, indem du eine These/ einen Aussagesatz schreibst.
  Vermeide „I think" im Text!
  Beispiel: *Although the advantages outweigh the disadvanges, a clique can be dangerous if the wrong people are in it.* ■

121 a) Write the main part of your essay using the arguments you have chosen. Remember that every argument has its own paragraph with a topic sentence and supporting sentences. For good style, use connecting phrases. Leave some space for the introduction.

b) Now read the Step up!-Box **above**. Then write the introduction to your argument.

c) Read the Step up!-Box **below**. Then write the conclusion to your essay. Give your essay a title.

Step up!

Aufbau eines Schlusses

Der **Schluss (*conclusion*)** beinhaltet eine abschließende Aussage über das Thema. Hier sollst du deine Meinung zu dem Thema bzw. dem *statement* darstellen.

Du kannst zum Beispiel

- nochmals das für dich entscheidende Argument für deine Position nennen oder
- einen Blick in die Zukunft werfen.

WICHTIG:
Im Schluss dürfen keine neuen Argumente auftauchen!

Eine mögliche Formulierung für den Schluss ist: "All in all one can say …" ■

122 You have read an article in an American newspaper saying *"animals should not be kept in zoos"*. What do you think? Write about 300 words. You may use a dictionary.

123 You have read an article in a British newspaper saying *"students should not bring their mobile phones to school"*.
What do you think? Write about 300 words.

Topic 36: Strategien zum Schreiben

124 In diesem Kapitel hast du verschiedene Strategien verwendet, um Texte zu Schreiben und zu Strukturieren. Suche die Strategien in den *Step up!*–Kästen des Kapitels und trage sie in die folgende Tabelle ein. Du musst entscheiden, ob es sich um eine Strategie handelt, die du vor dem Schreiben, während des Schreibens oder danach anwendest.

Writing Strategies
Vor dem Schreiben: ➡ sich in die Situation versetzen (S. 106) ➡ ➡ ➡ ➡ Für Zusammenfassung: Text in Sinnabschnitte gliedern, Teilüberschriften erstellen
Während des Schreibens: ➡ für Beschreibungen ausdrucksstarke Adjektive, Adverbien und beschreibende Nebensätze verwenden (S. 108, 129) ➡ ➡ ➡
Nach dem Schreiben: ➡ Sprachrichtigkeit kontrollieren (z. B. Zeiten, Rechtschreibung, false friends, he/she/it „s" im simple present) ➡ Sprachstil prüfen (förmlich /persönlich) (S. 106) ➡ ➡

Vocabulary –
Vokabelverzeichnis

In dieser Liste findest du Vokabeln, die im Band verwendet wurden, die dir jedoch unter Umständen noch nicht bekannt sind.
Die Abkürzung „fam." bedeutet, dass dieses Wort nur in der Umgangssprache verwendet wird. „AE" heißt, dass es sich um amerikanisches Englisch handelt. „BE" zeigt an, dass es sich um britisches Englisch handelt.

according to – nach
(to) account for – betragen
(to) ache – schmerzen
acquaintance – Bekannte*r
advantage – Vorteil
advertisement – Werbung
(to) affect – beeinflussen
agitated – beunruhigt
amazing – erstaunlich
amount – Betrag
anger – Wut
annoyed – genervt
appearance – Erscheinung
appliance – Gerät
(to) apply – sich bewerben
appointment – Termin
(to) appreciate – schätzen
(to) argue – argumentieren; streiten
arrow – Pfeil
(to) apply for – sich um/auf etwas bewerben
ashamed of – beschämt
assembly point – Sammelpunkt
assistance – Hilfe
asylum – Asyl
autumn break – Herbstferien
awesome – großartig

bank holiday *(BE)* – gesetzlicher Feiertag
basement – Keller
(to) be at sb's disposal – jmd zur Verfügung stehen
(to) be on the prowl – auf der Jagd sein
(to) be replaced – ersetzt werden
(to) be supposed to – sollen; dafür da sein
behaviour – Verhalten
(to) belong – dazugehören
benefit – Vorteil, Nutzen
bewildered – verblüfft
bilingual – zweisprachig
bill – Rechnung
billion – Milliarde
(to) board – an Bord gehen
border patrol – Grenzschutz
bored – gelangweilt
brackets – Klammern
breath-taking – atemberaubend
building site – Baustelle
bulletin board *(AE)* – schwarzes Brett, Anzeigenbrett

calm – ruhig
caretaker *(BE)* – Hausmeister
casual – zufällig, flüchtig
ceremony – Zeremonie
check *(AE)* – Rechnung
chiselled – gemeißelt
circle – Kreis
(to) claim – fordern
climax – Höhepunkt
closet – Wandschrank
coach – *hier:* Kutsche
commercial ad – Werbeanzeige
competition – Wettbewerb
(to) compromise – einen Kompromiss schließen
concerned – betroffen, beunruhigt
confidence – Vertrauen, Zuversicht
confused – verwirrt
congratulate – gratulieren
consequence – Konsequenz
considerably – erheblich
consumer – Verbraucher*in
content – Inhalt
contrary – Gegenteil
(to) contribute to – beisteuern
contribution – Beitrag
(to) cope with – bewältigen
(to) cram – lernen, büffeln
craze – Mode
(to) creep – kriechen
(to) criticize – kritisieren
crosswalk *(AE)* – Zebrastreifen
(to) cruise – herumwandern, herumfahren
curious – neugierig
current – aktuell

(to) dare – wagen, sich trauen
daring – waghalsig, tollkühn
decrease – Rückgang
defence – Schutz, Verteidigung
delighted – erfreut
(to) deliver – etw liefern
(to) demand – fordern
demand – Forderung
(to) depend on – von etw abhängen
depressed – deprimiert
desperate – verzweifelt
destination – Ziel
(to) destroy – zerstören
(to) dial – wählen
(to) dip – eintauchen; durchhängen
(to) disappoint – enttäuschen
(to) discriminate (against sb) – (jemanden) diskriminieren
discrimination – Diskriminierung
dissatisfied – unzufrieden
(to) dive – tauchen
diverse – vielfältig
dot – Punkt
downright – völlig
driver's license – Führerschein
driver's permit *(AE, fam.)* – Führerschein
(to) drop – fallen
drop – Tropfen
dustbin *(BE)* – Mülleimer

effect	– Effekt, Einfluss	fair-weather friend	– Schönwetter-freund*in
embarrassment	– Beschämung	false	– falsch, gefälscht
(to) emerge	– auftauchen	(to) fan	– fächern, wedeln
emigrant	– Auswanderer	fear	– Angst
(to) encourage	– ermutigen	feast	– Festmahl
(to) endanger	– gefährden	(to) feature	– aufweisen
engine fan	– Triebwerk	ferry	– Fähre
enormously	– ungeheuer	fields day *(AE)*	– Sportfest
(to) enrich	– bereichern	(to) figure sth out	– etw herausfinden
(to) enrol	– sich einschreiben	fire-extinguisher	– Feuerlöscher
enthusiastic	– enthusiastisch	first aid	– erste Hilfe
envy	– Neid	flip	– Schlag, Klaps
erected	– aufgestellt	fluffy	– flauschig
equal	– gleich	frightened	– beängstigt
equality	– Gleichheit; Gleich-berechtigung	frustrated	– frustriert
establishment	– Unternehmen; Einrichtung	furious	– (sehr) wütend
(to) examine	– untersuchen	further	– weitere*r, weiteres
exceptional	– außergewöhnlich		
excited	– aufgeregt	(to) **g**asp	– nach Luft schnappen
excitement	– Aufregung	gear	– Ausrüstung
(to) exclude	– ausschließen	gender	– Geschlecht
exclusively	– ausschließlich	(to) get homesick	– Heimweh bekommen
exhausted	– erschöpft	(to) give sb a turn	– jmd einen Schrecken einjagen
expectation	– Erwartung	(to) glow	– glühen
(to) experience	– erleben	grade retention	– Sitzenbleiben
(to) expire	– ablaufen	grateful	– dankbar
(to) explore	– untersuchen	gravy	– Bratensoße
extensively	– umfangreich	green card	– Greencard, dauer-hafte Aufent-haltserlaubnis für die USA
(to) **f**ace sth	– etw ausgesetzt sein		
facility	– Einrichtung; Anlage		
fake	– gefälscht, falsch		
(to) fail	– versagen, scheitern		

(to) groan – ächzen, stöhnen
guideline – Richtlinie

habit – Angewohnheit
hallway – Flur
harmless – harmlos
harpoon – Harpune
harvest – Ernte
headmaster – Schulleiter*in
hesitant – zögerlich
(to) hesitate – zögern
(to) highlight – markieren
highway *(AE)* – Autobahn, Bundesstraße
(to) hit home – ankommen (eine Botschaft)
(to) hit it off *(fam.)* – sich gut verstehen
horrified – entsetzt

immense – riesig
impressed – beindruckt
impressive – beindruckend
(to) improve – verbessern
in charge – verantwortlich
in spite of – trotz
(to) include – beinhalten
incompetence – Inkompetenz
incompetent – unfähig
incredible – unglaublich
ineffective – ineffektiv, unwirksam
insecure – unsicher
insight – Einsicht
insurance – Versicherung
instant – unmittelbar
instead of – anstatt
intensely – äußerst
intolerable – unerträglich
involvement – Beteiligung
irritated – gereizt

janitor *(AE)* – Hausmeister
jealousy – Eifersucht
jewel – Juwel
joy – Freude
joyful – fröhlich
jug – Krug

(to) keep in touch – in Verbindung bleiben
(to) kneel down – sich hinknien

laboratory – Labor
license plate *(AE)* – Nummernschild
lie – Lüge
lighter – Feuerzeug
limited – befristet
(to) line up *(AE)* – anstehen, Schlange stehen
located – gelegen
(to) lose one's temper – die Geduld verlieren
luau – Hawaianische Feier

mad – wütend
major – groß, bedeutend, wichtig
majority – Mehrheit
mane – Mähne
mangrove – Mangrove (Tropenbaum)
mankind – die Menschheit
marine stinger – Würfelqualle
(to) marvel – wundern

marvellous	– fabelhaft, wunderbar
mashed potatoes	– Kartoffelbrei
mate	– Kumpel*ine
measure	– Maßnahme
minor	– unbedeutend
minority	– Minderheit
miserable	– elend
(to) mold *(AE)*, mould *(BE)*	– formen, modellieren
(to) monitor	– beobachten
motorway *(BE)*	– Autobahn
multicultural	– multikulturell
myth	– Mythos
naïve	– naiv
network	– Netzwerk
nosy	– neugierig
notice board *(BE)*	– schwarzes Brett, Anzeigenbrett
number plate *(BE)*	– Nummernschild
obvious	– offensichtlich
(to) occur	– sich ereignen
odd	– merkwürdig
(to) operate	– betätigen
operator	– Betreiber*in
outsider	– Außenseiter*in
outward	– äußere*r, äußeres
owl	– Eule
pajama pants	– Pyjamahose
patient	– geduldig
(to) pay off	– sich auszahlen
pea	– Erbse
peak	– Spitze
peer pressure	– Gruppenzwang
penalty	– Strafe
penfriend	– Brieffreund*in
period of time	– Zeitspanne
permanent resident	– jmd mit dauerhafter Aufenthaltserlaubnis
personality	– Persönlichkeit
pervert	– Perverse*r
plain	– Fläche
plantation	– Plantage
plenty of	– eine Menge
polite	– höflich
(to) pose a question	– eine Frage stellen
prayer	– Gebet
prejudiced	– befangen, vorurteilsbehaftet
prematurely	– vorzeitig
presence	– Anwesenheit
pressure	– Druck
(to) pretend	– vorgeben
pretence	– Vortäuschung
previous	– vorhergehend
privacy	– Privatsphäre
(to) profit	– profitieren
prohibited	– verboten
(to) promise	– versprechen
prospects	– Perspektiven, Möglichkeiten
proud (of)	– stolz (auf)
(to) prove	– beweisen, belegen
(to) provide	– anbieten
psychologist	– Psychologe/Psychologin
public place	– öffentlicher Platz
puzzled	– verwirrt

(to) queue up (BE)	– anstehen, Schlange stehen
racism	– Rassismus
racist	– Rassist*in
(to) raffle off	– verlosen
rage	– Wut; Getöse
(to) realize	– sich klarwerden, erkennen
reassured	– beruhigt
recreational holiday	– Erholungsurlaub
(to) register	– anmelden
regret	– Bedauern
relieved	– erleichtert
(to) renovate	– renovieren
(to) replace	– ersetzen
responsible	– verantwortungsbewusst; verantwortlich
restless	– unruhig
rigid	– steif
(to) roast	– braten
(to) roll in money	– im Geld schwimmen
rude	– unfreundlich
run-down	– heruntergekommen
sadness	– Trauer
safety	– Sicherheit
sales clerk (AE)	– Verkäufer*in
sales manager	– Vertriebsleiter*in
(to) scan	– überfliegen
scare story (fam.)	– Gruselgeschichte
scenery	– Landschaft
seashore	– Strand
season	– Jahreszeit

secure	– sicher
(to) seethe	– kochen
seldom	– selten
(to) select	– auswählen
self-confidence	– Selbstbewusstsein
sense of hearing	– Hörsinn
senseless	– sinnlos, unsinnig
sensible	– vernünftig
sequel	– Fortsetzung
serious	– ernsthaft
(to) set	– hier: untergehen
several	– einige
share	– Anteil
(to) share	– teilen
(to) shrug	– zucken; die Schultern zucken
significance	– Bedeutung
(to) sink	– sinken
slice	– Scheibe
solstice	– Sonnwende
spectacular	– spektakulär
(to) spill	– verschütten, gießen
(to) smuggle	– schmuggeln
smuggler	– Schmuggler*in
spirit	– Geist, Seele
(to) spread	– sich ausbreiten; (sich) verbreiten
stadium	– Stadion
(to) stand at attention	– strammstehen
stockings	– Strümpfe
strength	– Stärke
(to) strike	– zuschlagen
(to) stroll	– bummeln
stuff	– Zeug
success	– Erfolg
(to) suffer	– leiden

suitable – passend
summer solstice – Sommersonnwende
sunrise – Sonnenaufgang
supervisor – Aufsichtsperson
supportive – unterstützend
survival – Überleben
suspicious – misstrauisch; verdächtig
swing – Schaukel

tactical – taktisch
temporary – vorübergehend
thrilled – begeistert
thrilling – aufregend
tight – eng, engmaschig
trash can *(AE)* – Mülltonne
(to) tremble – zittern
(to) trickle – tröpfeln
truancy – Schwänzen
trunk – *hier:* Stamm
tuition – *hier:* Unterricht
(to) tutor – unterrichten

uneasy – besorgt
unique – einzigartig
unskilled – ungelernt
upgraded – verbessert
upper floor – Obergeschoss
upset – aufgebracht
utterly – vollkommen

valuable – wertvoll
value – Nutzen, Wert
(to) vanish – verschwinden
various – verschieden
(to) vary – variieren, schwanken
vet – Tierarzt, Tierärztin
(to) vet – überprüfen
victim – Opfer
violence – Gewalt

waffles – Waffeln
waste of time – Zeitverschwendung
weakness – Schwäche
(to) weep – schluchzen
(to) whisper – flüstern
wilderness – Wildnis
witty – witzig, geistreich

zebra crossing – Zebrastreifen

Key –
Lösungen zu den Aufgaben

- Damit du sie schnell findest, wurden viele Lösungen farbig hervorgehoben.
- Beachte, dass es oft mehr als nur eine einzige richtige Antwort gibt. Die verschiedenen Möglichkeiten sind durch Schrägstriche voneinander getrennt, in Klammern stehende Wörter oder Satzteile können entfallen.
- Die Lösungen bei Textproduktion oder Sprachmittlung sind oft als Vorschlag zu verstehen. Lass dich deshalb nicht entmutigen, wenn dein Text von dem hier angegebenen Lösungsvorschlag abweicht.

Reading

Topic 1: Dealing with unknown words

1

	word family	other languages	context	German translation
out of necessity	☑ necessary	☐	☐	*aus Notwendigkeit*
simultaneously	☑ simultaneous	☑ *dt.: simultan*	☐	*gleichzeitig*
frustrated	☐	☑ *dt.: frustriert*	☐	*frustriert*
relocate	☐	☐	☑	*versetzen*
in mourning	☑ to mourn sb	☐	☑	*in Trauer*
unexpectedly	☑ to expect sth	☐	☐	*unerwartet*
deaf	☐	☐	☑	*taub*
profitable	☑ profit	☑ *dt.: profitabel*	☐	*profitabel*

2

False friend? (Yes / No)

a)
- She has hardly worked for the exam. – *Sie hat hart für die Prüfung gearbeitet.* — Yes ☑ No ☐

  correction: *Sie hat kaum für die Prüfung gearbeitet. (hart gearbeitet* = worked hard)

- The doctor gave him a receipt. – *Der Arzt gab ihm ein Rezept.* — Yes ☑ No ☐

  correction: *Der Arzt gab ihm eine Quittung. (Rezept =* prescription)

- The baker got up early. – *Der Bäcker stand früh auf.* — Yes ☐ No ☑

- He always spends a lot of money. – *Er spendet immer viel Geld.* ☑ ☐

  correction: *Er gibt immer viel Geld aus. (spenden* = to donate)
- The documentary about snakes is interesting. – *Der Dokumentarfilm über Schlangen ist interessant.* ☐ ☑
- She's really brave. – *Sie ist wirklich brav.* ☑ ☐

  correction: *Sie ist wirklich mutig. (brav* = well-behaved)
- He is also a good friend of mine. – *Er ist also ein guter Freund von mir.* ☑ ☐

  correction: *Er ist auch ein guter Freund von mir. (also* = thus)
- She can run fast for 5 kilometres. – *Sie kann fast 5 Kilometer lang rennen.* ☑ ☐

  correction: *Sie kann 5 Kilometer schnell rennen. (fast* = almost)

False friend — Yes / No

b)
- *Ich möchte dich nicht blamieren.* – ~~I don't want to blame you.~~ ☑ ☐

  correction: I don't want **to make you look stupid**.
  (to blame sb = *jemanden beschuldigen)*
- *Er stand in der Nähe der Boxen.* – ~~He was standing close to the boxes.~~ ☑ ☐

  correction: He was standing close to the **loudspeakers.**
  (boxes = *Kisten)*
- *Ich würde gerne ein Instrument spielen.* – I would like to play an instrument. ☐ ☑
- *In der Schule wird er gemobbt.* – ~~He is mobbed at school.~~ ☑ ☐

  correction: He is **bullied** at school.
  (to mob sb = *jemanden umringen)*
- *Das hat er wohl überhört.* – ~~Obviously he has overheard it.~~ ☑ ☐

  correction: Obviously he has **not heard** it.
  (to overhear sth – *belauschen/zufällig mithören)*
- *Sei still.* – ~~Be still.~~ ☑ ☐

  correction: Be **quiet**. (still = *immer noch; ruhig, im Sinne von unbewegt)*

Topic 2: Signs around the world

			true	false	not given
3	a)	Marine stingers can seriously hurt swimmers.			✓
	b)	During the summer months people are not allowed to swim there.		✓	
4	a)	If you jump from the cliff, you may get badly hurt.	✓		
	b)	If you need to be rescued, you will have to pay $150.			✓
5	a)	The sign is at the top of Africa's highest mountain.	✓		
	b)	Uhuru is an active volcano.			✓
6	a)	The sign warns travellers not to get close to the "Min Min Light".		✓	
	b)	No one knows where this light comes from.	✓		
7	a)	The signs inform you where you are standing.	✓		
	b)	They have been put up on the Equator.		✓	
	c)	On the opposite side of the earth is Perth, Australia.		✓	
8	a)	Students are not allowed inside this building.		✓	
	b)	Students who stay away from class will have to pay a fine.			✓
9	a)	The sign addresses people playing golf.		✓	
	b)	It tells people to be careful of cars crossing.		✓	

Topic 3: Study and travel

10 a)
- ☐ a newspaper article
- ☐ a brochure
- ☑ an advert
- ☐ a catalogue

b)
- ☐ explain how students can learn best a foreign language.
- ☑ make the reader book a language course.
- ☐ make children learn their vocabulary in groups rather than alone.
- ☐ give information about different countries and cultures.

c) *Mögliche Lösung:*

☐	passive	☑	active
☑	vocabulary	☐	party
☑	teacher	☐	catalogue
☐	alone	☑	youthful

11 a) Paragraph needed: **2** Keyword in the text: **effective**
relaxed atmosphere / **small (motivated) groups / friendly teachers / live in the country / use language outside classroom / real communication**

b) Paragraph needed: **3** Keywords in the text: **why travel with us**
meet other young people / experience new cultures / youthful and motivated teachers / experienced organisation / best value for money

c) Paragraph needed: **4** Keyword in the text: **language**
English / French / German / Italian / Spanish

d) Paragraph needed: **4** Keyword in the text: **destination, £**
Florence – from £290

e) Paragraph needed: **5** Keywords in the text: **call […] staff**
telephone, (send) e-mail

Topic 4: Whale watching

12

1	2	3	4	5	6	7	8	9	10	11	12
G	H	K	B	E	A	C	F	I	J	L	D

G TOM: Hi Phil, how are you? Long time no see. I've just returned from a trip to Australia.

H PHIL: Wow, that sounds interesting. I've never been to Australia. What did you enjoy most?

K TOM: That's a tough question. But I think the whale watching tour that we did off the east coast was the most exciting part of our trip.

B PHIL: Whale watching! Isn't that dangerous?

E TOM: Well, it can be. But if you travel with a responsible operator, they make sure that you're safe. You mustn't get too close to the animals because they're so huge, they might destroy the boat with a flip of their tail.

A PHIL: Oh, I'm afraid you got me wrong there … I wasn't thinking of your safety but of the whales. I guess they must get pretty annoyed or even scared if people come close to them and follow them with their boats.

C TOM: Oh, I see what you mean, but I think you've got it wrong. As I said, we didn't get close. We stopped about 200 metres from the whales and just watched them from a distance. And then – you won't believe this – they came closer to us. They really seemed curious to explore our boat and they even dived underneath it. That was really an exciting moment, and probably dangerous too, but it all seemed pretty safe at the time.

F PHIL: Well, that certainly sounds great and a little scary as well. Still, I'm not so sure. Your presence could affect the whales in ways we don't realise. I mean, the noise of the boat or the people must be terrible for the whales because they have such a fine sense of hearing.

I TOM: You've probably got a point there. But our crew told us not to make any loud noises and they really checked that people were behaving in the right way once we were close to the whales. The captain even turned off the motor. Plus, I guess people who have the opportunity to meet whales will never want to hurt them because they will appreciate their beauty much more. They might even help to protect them.

J PHIL: On second thoughts, tours like that might even help to save whales because the people realise that you can earn more money by showing tourists living whales than by hunting and killing them.

L TOM: Absolutely. So maybe you should try it yourself one day.

D PHIL: I'll see. If ever I happen to travel to the US or Australia, I'll think about it. OK, now I have to run. I have an appointment at the doctor's. See you.

13

Arguments against whale watching	Arguments for whale watching
• dangerous for animals and people • animals are followed/annoyed/scared • noise hurts whales' sense of hearing	• if you behave correctly, it is safe • if you behave correctly, the animals are fine • tourists admire beauty of whales → want to save them • tours help people to earn a living → don't need to hunt and kill whales

14 Keywords and their equivalents are highlighted in the table.

Statements	Words from the text
It's difficult for Tom to decide what he liked best about his trip to Australia.	That's a tough question. (Paragraph K)
Whales can damage ships easily.	… destroy the boat with a flip of their tale. (Pa. E)
Tom misunderstood Phil.	… you got me wrong … (Pa. A)
Tom felt secure on the ship.	… it all seemed pretty safe … (Pa. C)
Whales can hear very well.	… they have such a fine sense of hearing. (Par. F)
Phil is considering doing whale watching himself one day.	… I'll think about it. (Pa. D)
Phil is in a hurry.	… now I have to run. (Pa. D)

15
- Choose a responsible tour operator.
- Keep your distance. / Don't get too close to the whales.
- Don't make any unnecessary noises. / Be quiet when (you are) close to the whales.

Topic 5: Summer camp

16
- The text is a blog.
- A boy, Michael, is writing an online diary about his stay at a summer camp (in British Columbia).
- On the pictures you can see that he goes kayaking, climbing …
- He will probably tell the reader about his experience at the summer camp, about what he likes and dislikes and about the people he meets there.

17

C	D	F	A
privacy Privatsphäre	survival skills Überlebens- techniken	What a drag! Wie langweilig	wilderness Wildnis

K	H	B
lighter Feuerzeug	ache weh tun	exhausted erschöpft

Hinweise:

A **wilderness** – *Wildnis:*
Du kennst das Adjektiv „wild“ und an der Endung „-ness“ erkennst du, dass es sich hier um ein Nomen handelt. Das deutsche Wort „Wildnis“ hört sich ähnlich an.

B **exhausted** – *erschöpft:*
Du kannst aus dem Zusammenhang schließen, dass Michael von der Tour sehr müde und erschöpft ist, denn er muss sich viel ausruhen.

C **privacy** – *Privatsphäre:*
Du kennst das englische Adjektiv „private“ und natürlich das deutsche Wort „privat“. An der Endung „-cy“ kannst du erkennen, dass es sich hier um ein Nomen handelt.

D **survival skills** – *Überlebenstechniken:*
Du kennst das Verb „(to) survive“. Aus der folgenden Beschreibung dessen, was Michael lernt, kannst du erschließen, was es im Zusammenhang mit „skill“ bedeutet.

F **What a drag!** – *Wie langweilig*:
Du kannst aus dem Zusammenhang erkennen, dass der Ausdruck negativ gemeint ist und dass Michael seine drei Zimmergenossen nicht beneidet.

H **(to) ache** – *weh tun:*
Du kennst Wörter wie „headache“, „toothache“ oder „stomach ache“. Hier wird „ache“ als Verb verwendet.

K **lighter** – *Feuerzeug:*
Du kennst das Nomen „light“ und sicherlich auch das Verb „to light“, vielleicht sogar den Ausdruck „to light a fire“. Auch aus dem Zusammenhang kannst du die Bedeutung erraten, denn Michael hat zwar gelernt, ein Feuer ohne moderne Hilfsmittel anzuzünden, dennoch nimmt er ein Feuerzeug mit.

18 Satzteile, die etwas über Michaels Gefühle aussagen, sind farbig markiert.

Day 1
Today I arrived at the summer camp in British Columbia, Canada. I was very excited because it was the first time that I had been on a plane trip on my own. When I arrived in Vancouver, a guy from the camp picked me and some other teenagers up and took us to the camp.
When I saw my room, I was pretty annoyed because I have to share the room with three other boys. Man, that's tough because it means that I won't have any privacy for the next two weeks.

Day 3
The other boys in my room are quite OK. Sometimes it's a bit hard to communicate because they come from Mexico, Brazil and Italy. But, hey, I'm the lucky one really because José, Miguel and Antonio have got English lessons five days a week, three hours a day. What a drag! And I thought this was a holiday camp! Well, it is for me. I'm outdoors most of the day and go swimming or play soccer and yesterday I also tried golf. It's harder than it looks, really. The food here is nice and the other guys are mostly pretty cool. I spend a lot of time with Carl. He's from Florida and we've become mates, kind of.

Day 5

I'm getting bored. Mum and I agreed that I could do the "Adventure Tour" and they promised kayaking and rock climbing, but so far we're only preparing for the big trip. The trainers keep telling us we need to get ready "for the real thing". So I have to learn survival skills, like what to do when we see a bear, which wild berries to eat, how to make a fire and so on. I'll take my lighter anyway, just in case. We also learn about first aid and do a lot of planning, like what gear to select, what clothes and shoes to pack and what food to take along.

Day 6

Another day of planning our trip but, hey, now we're done. Tomorrow we'll be off into the wilderness. I'm really looking forward to this. My backpack is pretty heavy so I hope we won't have to walk for too many miles. Tonight I'll try to get some more sleep because we're leaving pretty early. Carl will come, too.

Day 13

Man, that was great. It was really worth all the preparation. We spent five days in the wilderness and went rock climbing, kayaking and mountain biking. We returned yesterday but I was so exhausted that I had to rest for a day before I felt like doing anything at all. It was incredible, the scenery was just brilliant and the rock climbing was extremely cool. But now I'm aching all over… Phew, I'll have to rest some more and then I need to pack my bag because tomorrow I'll be on my way home again. What a pity.

19

a) **He is excited because everything is new to him. When he sees his room, he is annoyed because he wants more privacy.**

b) **He is getting bored because he has to practice, prepare and plan a lot before he is allowed to go on the "Adventure Tour".**

c) **He is exhausted but also very happy and impressed by the trip. / He is aching all over after five days in the wilderness but he enjoyed the activities and the beauty of nature.**

d) **He is quite sorry and sad that his holidays are over and he has to return home.**

Topic 6: Amit, an undocumented immigrant

20 *(Lösungsvorschlag)*
The text is interesting for my project. The phrases "undocumented immigrant" (headline), "ten years old" and "California" and the picture of the American flag show that it fits my topic.

21 A young immigrant from Sri Lanka …
- [ ] is found to be an illegal resident in the USA.
- [x] tells of his experience as an undocumented immigrant in the USA.
- [ ] moves to the USA with his family and grows up there.
- [ ] tries to get hold of a fake Green Card to be able to get his driver's license.

22

paragraph	1	2	3	4	5	6
headline	D	G	A	H	B	E

23 a) Why did Amit have to leave his home?
- [ ] His grandparents wanted him to come and live with them.
- [x] His parents hoped he would have a better life in the USA.
- [ ] His uncle took him with him to the USA.
- [ ] His father had died in an accident.

b) How did Amit's grandpa support the family?
- [ ] He registered Amit with the local police in the USA.
- [ ] He got Amit's father a job after his accident.
- [ ] He paid for Amit's ticket to the USA.
- [x] He sent them money to Sri Lanka.

c) How does Amit learn that he is an undocumented immigrant?
- [ ] His classmates show him their driver's license.
- [ ] A clerk tells him that his driver's license is fake.
- [x] His grandpa tells him that his papers are false.
- [ ] Amit finds out that his Green Card has expired.

Topic 7: Studying abroad

24 a) Useful information: headline, layout, many numbers
The text is a newspaper article. It is about students that come to Australia to study there. There are many facts and numbers given.

b) Who do you think the text might interest?

- [ ] Young people who want to study in China
- [ ] Math teachers in China
- [x] Young people who want to study in Australia
- [ ] English teachers in the USA

25

lines	headline
ll. 1–7	Advantages for Australia
ll. 8–10	**Advantages for international students**
ll. 11–15	**How to become an international student in Australia**
ll. 16–26	**Where international students come from**
ll. 27–29	**How old they are**
ll. 30–33	**What sex they are**
ll. 34–51	**Australian students abroad**

26 a)

percentage	country of origin in 2014
34 %	China
almost 10 %	India
5 %	**Malaysia**

b)

male	female	country of origin
54 %	46 %	overall
63 %		Nepal
	62 %	USA

27

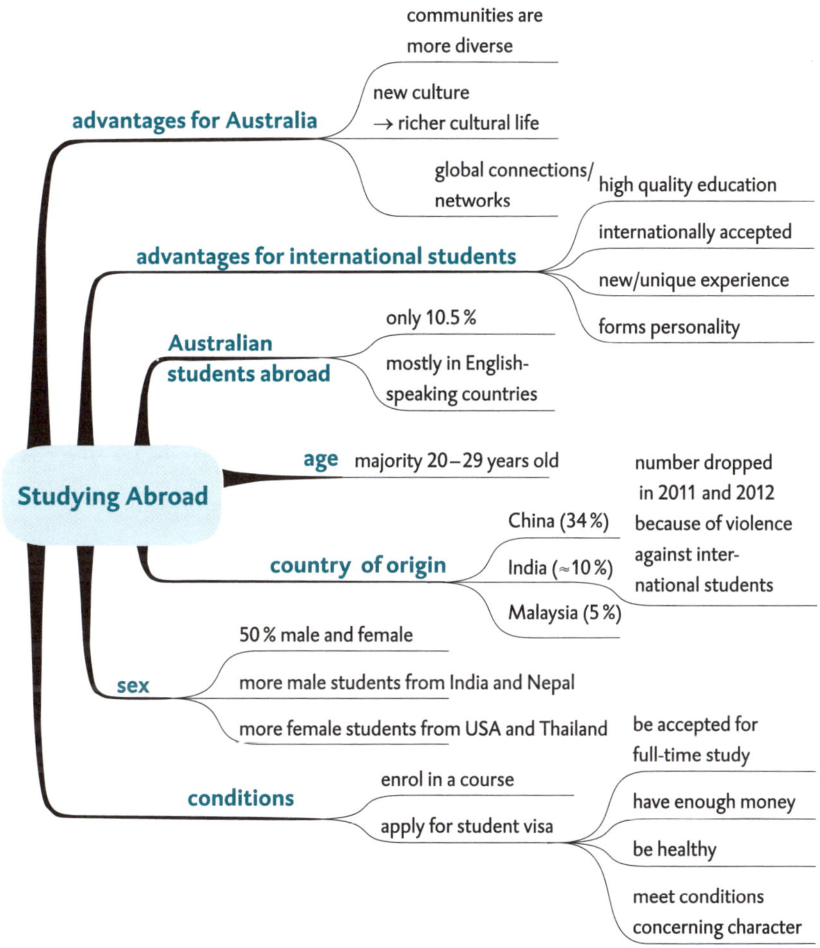
Studying Abroad
advantages for Australia
communities are more diverse
new culture → richer cultural life
global connections/ networks
advantages for international students
high quality education
internationally accepted
new/unique experience
forms personality
Australian students abroad
only 10.5 %
mostly in English-speaking countries
age
majority 20–29 years old
country of origin
China (34 %)
India (≈10 %)
number dropped in 2011 and 2012 because of violence against international students
Malaysia (5 %)
sex
50 % male and female
more male students from India and Nepal
more female students from USA and Thailand
conditions
enrol in a course
apply for student visa
be accepted for full-time study
have enough money
be healthy
meet conditions concerning character

Topic 8: Chat rooms

28 a) ☑ "Skim" the text (see Topic 6). b) ☑ Take notes while reading.
☑ Underline keywords.

c)

Who?	Amy and her mother
Where?	in Amy's room, at her computer
When?	some days after Amy met Zed on the Internet, in the evening
What?	they discuss the danger of chat rooms, Amy tells her mum about Zed, her mother worries about Amy
Why?	Amy has no one else to talk to, Amy's mother is worried that Amy spends too much time on her computer, has no friends, might meet a pervert on the Internet

29 What do you learn about …

Amy:	• is aware of the dangers of chatrooms but isn't worried about the Internet • is a bit naïve → believes that supervisors can protect users • met a boy (Zed) online; thinks about him • her webname is "Buzybee" • likes Zed → talk about a lot of things • has no friends to talk to → needs to talk to her mother • lies to her mum to get rid of her
Amy's mother:	• had penfriends when she was young • nosy/curious → observes what her daughter does on the computer • is suspicious of the Internet • is worried her daughter might meet a pervert on the Internet • thinks Zed is too old for Amy • doesn't believe what Zed says about himself • is worried because Amy has no friends • is worried because Amy spends too much time on the computer/ indoors
Zed:	• Amy's online friend • claims to be 18 years old • says he is a kind of sales manager in an office

30

	Statements	True	False	Lines in the text
a)	Friends on the Internet answer quickly.	✓	☐	ll. 3–5
b)	Amy's mum often looks over her daughter's shoulder to see what she is doing online.	✓	☐	ll. 5–8
c)	Amy thinks that newspaper articles about chat rooms are made to frighten people.	✓	☐	l. 16
d)	Amy always enters her date of birth when she is online.	☐	✓	
e)	There is someone to ensure that the rules on a chat room are followed.	✓	☐	l. 28
f)	Amy's mother manages to make her daughter start to doubt chat room safety.	✓	☐	l. 31
g)	Amy's mother thinks there are too many people in a chat room to be controlled.	✓	☐	l. 32
h)	Zed, Amy's friend, works in a shop.	☐	✓	
i)	Amy's mother is happy that Amy has found a new friend.	☐	✓	
j)	Amy's mother wants her daughter to go outside.	✓	☐	ll. 64–67

Topic 9: Life is an open door

31 *(Lösungsvorschlag)*

Open door:

- We have many possibilities and opportunities in life.
- We can choose what we want to do in life.

Closed door:

- Many things which we cannot influence have an effect on our life, e. g. our nationality, colour of our skin, family, sex, religion.
- People are prejudiced.

32 a)

A	B	C	D	E	F	G	H
2	4	6	7	1	3	8	5

b) *(Lösungsvorschlag)*
The poem is about life and the possibilities it offers. This is shown by the fact that the word "life" is used five times in the poem and once in its title. Life is compared to different objects, e. g. an open door or a highway. These stand for the possibilities that life offers.

33 *(Lösungsvorschlag)*

sense unit (lines)	image
ll. 1–2	open door
ll. 3–4	highway
ll. 5–7	plain, arrow (which life is not)
ll. 8–10	open door

34 *(Lösungsvorschlag)*

image (lines)	what it tells you about life
open door ll. 1–2	Life offers different opportunities which we may or may not use depending on our "talents".
highway ll. 3–4	It goes on for a long time ("a highway running") if we do not die young either because of an illness or a fatal accident ("by chance"). We may also end life early by committing suicide (exit life "prematurely, at will").
≠plain, arrow ll. 5–7	Life holds surprises and during a lifetime it may take some unexpected turns, for example because of certain events. There will always be good times but also bad ones. Life is not "flat" or "straight".
open door ll. 9–10	However, life is still an open door offering many opportunities. Even though we do not know what the future brings ("open to a future untold"), we can influence it ("a future that we can mold").

Topic 10: Strategien zum Leseverstehen

35 *(Lösungsvorschlag)*

Reading-Strategies
Vor dem Lesen: ➡ Vermutungen über den Text anstellen (z. B. S. 9) ➡ Bilder und Überschrift nutzen (z. B. S. 9) ➡ Textsorte erkennen (S. 9) ➡ Wortschatz aktivieren (S. 9) ➡ Schlüsselwörter in der Aufgabe markieren (S. 11)
Während des Lesens: ➡ Scannen/Schlüsselbegriffe markieren (S. 11) ➡ Textstellen markieren (z. B. S. 14) ➡ zwischen den Zeilen lesen (S. 19) ➡ Skimmen/Text überfliegen (z. B. S. 20) ➡ Text in Sinnabschnitte gliedern/Teilüberschriften erstellen (S. 25)
Wenn ich Wörter nicht verstehe: ➡ Ignorieren (S. 2) ➡ Wortfamilien (S. 2) ➡ andere Sprachen (S. 2) ➡ Aus dem Kontext erschließen (S. 2) ➡ Wörterbuch (S. 2)
Nach dem Lesen: ➡ Textzusammenfassung ➡ Informationen in Tabelle ergänzen (S. 14) ➡ Mindmap erstellen (S. 25) ➡ Die W-Fragen beantworten (S. 27)

Listening

Topic 11: Plans for the weekend

Listening text 1: Weather forecast

Track 01

Hello everybody, and welcome to "Thank God it's Friday" here on CBA. And this is our weekend weather forecast for Little Rock, Arkansas. Right now it is raining heavily and it will go on raining till tonight. This afternoon you'd best stay inside and do whatever needs to be done. So tidy up or do your homework because then you're free for the weekend when the weather will be much better. Still, we're rather lucky because in the northeast of the US it's all snow coming down. But here in Little Rock it's warm – pretty warm for the season actually. Maximum temperature today is 57. Tonight we expect fair skies and then the temperature will drop to 48.

Saturday will be much better at just 62 degrees but a lot of sunshine. The chance of rain is going down to zero percent, so Saturday is the day to spend outside. We suggest a long walk with your dog if you have one. Else, take some friends along and enjoy the sun. Lowest temperatures will be at 46 – quite a warm night if you want to go out.

Sunday will be a bit warmer again at 66 degrees, but it will be partly cloudy. Under the clouds the night will be incredibly warm. Temperatures won't sink below 52 degrees. So, believe it or not, we suggest a nice barbecue for Sunday afternoon, even in February. Especially as the warm temperatures will bring along some stormy days next week. More on that tomorrow.

Listening text 2: Time for commercials

Track 02

1. "Knights of Empires" is out now. The sequel to the award-winning and best-selling strategy game "Kings of Empires". King Henry's empire is under attack. You need to make the right tactical move and make clever economic decisions to protect the empire. Get the CD or app now or play online with or against other players. Long live the Empire!
2. This weekend Little Rock Super Mall opens 48 hours for you. Come and enjoy a relaxed evening in a great atmosphere. Take your time to stroll through the various stores and find everything from thrilling books to the latest TV sets, from the hottest designer shoes to comfortable furniture. In-between, enjoy a delicious meal in one of our various restaurants or have a drink at the cocktail bar. Starting tonight at 8 p.m. we will only close again

on Sunday night at 8 p.m. So come and enjoy yourselves at Little Rock's favorite shopping mall.

3. You're looking for adventure? You love nature? Then come to Costa Rica. Here you'll find huge mangrove forests, active volcanoes and coffee and banana plantations. Costa Rica is small, so distances are short but the variety of its fauna and flora is immense. Listen to the sound of monkeys and birds while you relax at one of our beautiful beaches or take a tour into the forest and climb a volcano. For more information go to "holidays-in-costa-rica.com".

Listening text 3: Events at Little Rock

Track 03

Finally, it's Friday afternoon and for those of you who still need to come up with some last minute plans for the weekend, here are some ideas for you. This weekend there are some really great events going on in Little Rock. So we picked the most amazing three for you.

Our first event is Gabriel Iglesias, better known as "fluffyguy". He became widely known with his program "I'm not fat … I'm fluffy". And he is sure to deliver a smart and electrifying comedy experience tomorrow night. His show starts at 8 p.m. at the Robinson Center Exhibit Hall. Gabriel Iglesias mixes storytelling, parodies and sound effects to share his funny experiences with us. Tickets are $ 52.70.

Next, we suggest the Harlem Globetrotters with their new program "Fans Rule!". I guess I needn't say much about the Harlem Globetrotters because everybody's heard of them and their athletic show, where they perform amazing moves and prove to be the world's greatest dribblers. You can see them tonight at half past eight at the Verizon Arena. So I expect to meet all basketball fans there tonight. Tickets start at $ 38.

Finally, this weekend's highlight in Little Rock. On Saturday night in the Robinson Center Music Hall, we present Pentatonix. You sure all know Pentatonix. They won the 3rd season of the Sing-Off on NBC with their a cappella arrangement of "Eye of the Tiger". On Saturday at 9 p.m. they'll present their latest CD with cover songs which are all arranged a cappella. The five singers are really impressive. So don't miss them! Unfortunately, the ticket prices are also impressive. Tickets are from $ 149 to $ 244, which is probably quite expensive for a last minute idea. That's why we're giving away two lots of two tickets for their show on Saturday at 9 p.m. at the Robinson Center Music Hall. If you want to win, call us and tell us which song started Pentatonix' success.

36 • From the title and the introduction, what kind of text do you expect?

- [ ] a podcast
- [x] a radio programme
- [x] a report
- [ ] a commercial ad

• What will the text be about?

- [x] the weather in the near future
- [ ] information on past events
- [ ] stories about celebrities
- [x] suggestions on what to do and what to wear in the next few days

• What do you know about the topic?

- [x] a forecast is a prediction of the future
- [ ] in a weather report they often talk about the past
- [ ] in the UK it rains all the time
- [x] in the US temperatures are given in Fahrenheit – not Celsius

• Which words do you already know to talk about the topic? Look at the following pictures and write down verbs, nouns and adjectives.

sun	thunderstorm
sunny/hot/warm	thunder
(to) shine	lightning
cloud	wind/storm
cloudy	windy/stormy
(to) cloud (up)	(to) blow
rain	snow/ice
rainy/wet	snowy/cold
(to) rain (heavily)	(to) snow/(to) fall

- Do you need to understand everything or just single words to do the next exercise?

  Im Prinzip musst du vor allem auf Details achten. Da ein Wetterbericht jedoch normalerweise sehr knapp ist und viele Informationen enthält, solltest du auch den Text als Ganzes verstanden haben. Es sind also beide Antworten richtig.

37 a)

	Friday	Saturday	Sunday
highest temperature (°F)	57	62	66
lowest temperature (°F)	48	46	52
weather	(heavy) rain	sunny; no rain	(partly) cloudy
suggested activities	stay inside; tidy up; do your homework	go for a walk (with your dog/ friends); enjoy the sun	have a BBQ

b) see a)

38 a)
- ads/adverts/advertisements, commercials
- about products or services consumers are meant to buy
- commercials can be about many different products, like cars, products for the household, e.g. washing powder, food, soft drinks, insurance
- lots of superlatives, e.g. latest, newest, best, biggest, greatest
- You just need to understand what product is advertised but not all the details.

b)
- "Knights of Empires", computer game, smartphone game/app
- Little Rock Super Mall/a big shopping mall (in Little Rock)
- Costa Rica/holidays in Costa Rica

39 a)
- short informative text
- tips for the weekend, information on cinema, concerts, theatre, etc.
- cinema, theatre, sport events, prices are given, time and place
- movies, plays, drama, exciting, funny, fantastic, expensive, cheap, dollars, tonight, tomorrow night, at 8 p.m., late night, concert hall, arena, stadium, theatre
- listening for details: single words, like numbers and names

b)

	Event 1	Event 2	Event 3
Who?	**Gabriel Iglesias "fluffyguy"**	**Harlem Globe-trotters**	**Pentatonix**
What?	**(stand-up) comedy**	**athletic show / basketball show**	**a capella group / concert**
What day?	**Saturday**	**Friday**	**Saturday**
Where?	Robinson Center in the "Exhibit **Hall**"	Verizon **Arena**	Robinson Center in the **"Music Hall"**
What time?	**8 p.m.**	**8.30 p.m.**	**9 p.m.**
Ticket price?	**$ 52.70**	**from $ 38**	**$ 149–244**

c) see b)

Topic 12: Planking, owling and milking – The latest web craze

Listening text 1

Track 04

It all started back in 1997 when two British teenagers, Gary Clarkson and Christian Langdon, were bored and therefore started the "lying down game". The rules are fairly easy. Imagine you're standing at attention, only that you're not standing but lying on the floor, your face down, arms rigid at your side, feet pointing to the ground. Nothing special really. That's probably why the game didn't spread beyond Clarkson and Langdon's circle of friends for the next ten years. However, in 2007 they started a Facebook group to publish their photos of the "lying down game". From then on it developed quite quickly, partly because of reports in the British media. The game went international and took on several names. In Australia it is called planking, in the USA and in Ireland facedowns. At its peak, the Facebook group got up to 1,000 new photos a day. The photos became more and more daring and crazy.

Listening text 2

Track 05

It all started back in 1997 when two British teenagers, Gary Clarkson and Christian Langdon, were bored and therefore started the "lying down game". The rules are fairly easy. Imagine you're standing at attention, only that you're not standing but lying on the floor, your face down, arms rigid at your side, feet pointing to the ground. Nothing special really. That's probably why the game didn't spread beyond Clarkson and Langdon's circle of friends for the next ten years. However, in 2007 they started a Facebook group to publish their photos of the "lying down game". From then on it developed quite quickly, partly because of reports in the British media. The game went international and took on several names. In Australia it is called planking, in the USA and in Ireland facedowns. At its peak, the Facebook group got up to 1,000 new photos a day. The photos became more and more daring and crazy. One photo shows an airport worker lying down inside the engine fan of a jet plane. People were looking for more and more spectacular locations to lie down and in 2011 the lying down game reached its sad climax when it claimed its first victim. In Brisbane, Australia, a 20-year-old man fell from a balcony on the seventh floor while planking and died at the scene.

Since then the number of new photos of planking or lying down has gone down but only to be replaced by other, equally senseless acts. For example, there has been "owling", which means that people sit like owls in unusual places and, of course, have a photo taken. Or "milking", which involves spilling the milk out of a bottle over one's head in a public place. The most stupid one yet may be "cat breading". Here, a slice of bread is placed around a cat's head to make it look like a little lion with a mane of bread. Maybe the latest trend is "Vadering", when people perform a copy of Darth Vader's typical move.

40 a)

A	B	C	D
6	4	3	1

b)

Who?	Gary Clarkson and Christian Langdon; two British teenagers	
Where?	Great Britain	
When?	1997	2007
What?	started lying down game	started a Facebook group
Why?	bored	publish photos

41 a)

- How long did the game take to spread?
  to spread = to become popular/known
- How did the game become internationally known?
  to become internationally known: to spread around the globe/ the world

- What is it called in Australia?
  called = its name, it is known as
  Australia = Down Under
- What is it called in Ireland?
  called = its name, it is known as
  Ireland = the Emerald Isle
- How did the photos published on Facebook change over time?
  photo = photograph, picture, snap, snapshot
- Where did the airport worker perform his act?
  airport worker = airport employee, man working at the airport
- What does the speaker think of these acts?
  think = to his mind, in his opinion, to believe
- Which is the latest web craze?
  latest = newest, most recent
  web = Internet
  craze = fashion, trend

b)
- How long did the game take to spread?
  10 years/from 1997 to 2007
- How did the game become internationally known?
  Facebook group/reports in British media
- What is it called in Australia?
  planking
- What is it called in Ireland?
  facedowns
- How did the photos published on Facebook change over time?
  more daring and crazy/more spectacular locations
- Where did the airport worker perform his act?
  inside engine fan (of plane)
- What does the speaker think of these acts?
  (thinks) they are stupid/useless/senseless (acts)
- Which is the latest web craze?
  Vadering

Topic 13: National Aboriginal Day

Listening text

Track 06

Hello everyone. My name is Kimberlee and I'll be your guide for the next two hours. To start with, I would like to congratulate you on your perfect timing. You've arrived just in time for the 11 days of Celebrate Canada, which will start the day after tomorrow and last for 11 days. There will be lots of events and activities for you to join and to learn more about Canada and its culture. No matter where you travel from here, you'll find that events are organised from coast to coast all over Canada. The first series of events will be on June 21st, when we celebrate National Aboriginal Day, and it ends with Canada Day on July 1st.

National Aboriginal Day is an opportunity to learn more about Aboriginal people and their contributions to Canada. In Canada there are about 1,500,000 First Nations, Métis and Inuit people. On National Aboriginal Day they will come together in many places to celebrate and share their rich and diverse cultures. You are invited to share in their experiences, stories, songs and spirit. Believe me, their traditional games and dances will bring you to your feet!

Most of the time, events include summer solstice festivals, because June 21st is the first day of summer. Here in Thunder Bay, for example, a sunrise ceremony will be held at 5.30 a.m. And for those who are willing to get up that early and to celebrate with us, there will be a traditional breakfast afterwards. For centuries, many first inhabitants have celebrated June 21st. It's the day of the year where it's light for the longest and which has the shortest night. That's why it became the official National Aboriginal Day in 1996.

So join the celebration while you're here and get a deeper insight into the cultural richness of First Nations, Inuit and Métis peoples. I promise that it'll be unforgettable.

Okay, now let's have a look around the place you're standing on. It is …

42 The text will describe how National Aboriginal Day is celebrated in Canada. It will also be about Canada Day, which is probably a day when the country is celebrated.

43 *(Lösungsvorschlag)*

nouns, names	further information
Celebrate Canada	starts day after tomorrow; 11 days; join, learn about Canada; lots of events (activities) are organised all over Canada
National Aboriginal Day	celebrated June 21st; learn about culture, first series of events; 1,500,000 Aboriginal people celebrate traditional games and dances
Canada Day	July 1st
summer solstice	first day of summer; June 21st; longest light – shortest night; National Aboriginal Day since 1996
Thunder Bay	get up early, at 5.30 a.m.; sunrise ceremony is held; traditional breakfast

44

	true	false	not given
a) Canadians will celebrate their country for 11 days.	✓		
b) Events are organised throughout the whole country.	✓		
c) National Aboriginal Day is the first event to be celebrated.	✓		
d) It will be followed by Canada Day the next day.		✓	
e) There are about 1,500,000 Inuit people in Canada.		✓	
f) Guests get actively involved in the activities.	✓		
g) In dance workshops people can learn traditional dances.			✓
h) The summer solstice marks the day with the fewest hours of light.		✓	
i) In Thunder Bay people are invited to watch the rising of the sun together on June 21st.	✓		
j) June 21st has been known as National Aboriginal Day since 1969.		✓	
k) Aboriginals had to fight for a long time to get their own National Day.			✓

Topic 14: Grade retention

Listening text 1

Track 07

ROGER: Hello, I'm Roger and this is my weekly show: "We want to know what you think". Each week we discuss a current topic and you can call, email or twitter us to tell us what you think. This week, our topic is grade retention, so we're asking students, parents and teachers to express their opinion.

Year after year about 250,000 students have to repeat a class. ...

Listening text 2

Track 08

ROGER: Hello, I'm Roger and this is my weekly show: "We want to know what you think". Each week we discuss a current topic and you can call, email or twitter us to tell us what you *** (1). This week, our topic is grade retention, so we're asking students, parents and teachers to express their *** (2).

Year after *** (3) about 250,000 students have to repeat a class. According to the latest studies, 16,500 teachers are needed to teach these students. We're talking about costs between 850 million and 1.2 billion *** (4) a year. So it's worth thinking about the pros and *** (5) of grade retention. While some teachers say that grade retention is a good way of helping students cope with expectations, school psychologists argue that grade retention is not only ineffective but also has *** (6) effects. Students who've had to repeat a class often feel incompetent and stupid. It's really bad for their self-*** (7) and they're often more likely to leave school altogether.

Listening text 3

Track 09

ROGER: Hello, I'm Roger and this is my weekly show: "We want to know what you think". Each week we discuss a current topic and you can call, email or twitter us to tell us what you think. This week, our topic is grade retention, so we're asking students, parents and teachers to express their opinion.

Year after year about 250,000 students have to repeat a class. According to the latest studies, 16,500 teachers are needed to teach these students. We're talking about costs between 850 million and 1.2 billion dollars a year. So it's worth thinking about the pros and cons of grade retention. While some teachers say that grade retention is a good way of helping students cope with expectations, school psychologists argue that grade retention is not only ineffective but also has negative effects. Students who've had to repeat a class often feel incompetent and stupid. It's really bad for their self-confidence and they're often more likely to leave school altogether.

Here's our first caller now.

SHANE: Hi, I'm Shane. I almost failed 8th grade but I worked very hard and was moved up into 9th grade. Now I'm doing fine and I think the pressure I was under last year was good for me. I really wanted to stay in my class with my friends. If it hadn't been for that pressure, I wouldn't have worked hard enough for school. So I think it's a good thing to tell students they might have to repeat a year because otherwise lots of us are simply too lazy.

ROGER: So obviously it worked for Shane, but then she didn't have to repeat a class after all.

KARL: Hi, I think that retention's unfair because it's mostly kids from poor families and Hispanic and African-American kids that are held back. The fact that they're often even held back more than once, shows that it doesn't help. At first they might do a bit better, but then they get new topics but still have the same problems. These kids need help when it comes to their learning style or maybe even with their problems at home. Grade retention doesn't help them at all. It just makes them feel useless.

ROGER: Okay, so there seems to be an equality problem as well. Next, we have a teacher on the line.

ALICE: Hello, I'm a teacher at an inner-city school and we have lots of students who need to do a year over. For some it's actually helpful but for most it's a waste of time. They're not motivated because they don't see why they should work harder at school because they don't believe in a good future anyway. I think the money we spend on grade retention should be used to really help these kids. We need people to tutor them more closely and we need to offer them goals for their future.

ROGER: Thank you for your calls and e-mails. Obviously, it's a very important topic that we should discuss in more detail. Before we end our show, I'd like Emily Button, school psychologist in New York, to give some advice to those of you who risk failing or have a child who might have to repeat a class. Emily, what advice can you give?

EMILY: According to the information we have, it's most important to include the parents. Parents, teachers and students need to work together. If possible, school specialists should be included, too. Parents need to talk to their kids' teachers about their strengths and weaknesses. Often, they're too hesitant and don't dare to ask questions, but they should ask what special support the school can offer to help students meet the expectations.

45 a) When a pupil has bad grades, he/she has to repeat a class. / Grade retention means that a pupil has failed a year at school and has to repeat it.

b) *(possible solution)*

1 **think/believe**

2 **opinion/view/point of view**

3 **year**

4 **dollars**

5 **cons**

6 **negative/dangerous**

7 **confidence**

46 a) Experts say that grade retention costs …

- ☐ up to $ 1.2 million a year.
- ☑ up to $ 1.2 billion a year.
- ☐ at least $ 1.2 million a year.
- ☐ at least $ 1.2 billion a year.

b) Who argues for grade retention?

- ☐ most students
- ☐ most school psychologists
- ☐ Roger, the radio reporter
- ☑ some teachers

c) School psychologists make a connection between grade retention and …

- ☐ where students and their parents come from.
- ☐ gender (girl or boy).
- ☐ success in later life.
- ☑ a feeling of incompetence.

d) The first caller thinks grade retention is helpful because …

- ☐ grade 8 is a difficult year.
- ☐ parents are afraid their children have to repeat a class.
- ☑ it makes students work harder.
- ☐ students are put under pressure by their friends.

e) The second caller thinks grade retention …
- [x] doesn't help with the real problems.
- [ ] doesn't even help for a short time.
- [ ] happens too often.
- [ ] happens to everybody.

f) The teacher who calls would like to use the money spent on grade retention to …
- [x] offer students better prospects for the future.
- [ ] pay teachers more money.
- [ ] spend more time with the students.
- [ ] pay for smaller classes.

g) In the end Roger talks to …
- [ ] a secondary school teacher.
- [ ] a student who has to repeat a class.
- [x] a school psychologist.
- [ ] a parent whose child is in danger of failing.

h) According to Emily Button it is most important that …
- [ ] specialists try to find out more about the issue.
- [x] parents know more about what their kids do at school.
- [ ] schools support students better.
- [ ] students know about their strengths and weaknesses.

47 *Arguments for grade retention:*
- helps students to cope with the expectations/to meet the expectations
- makes students work harder because they want to stay in their grade/ with their friends

Arguments against grade retention (only five arguments are needed):
- is bad for students' self-confidence → they feel incompetent and stupid
- has a negative effect on their school career because students who were retained are more likely to leave school
- is not fair because Hispanic and African-American children and children from poorer families are more likely to be retained

- it doesn't help students with their real problems, e.g. learning difficulties or problems at home
- it is a waste of time
- students aren't motivated to work hard at school because they do not have any hope for the future
- grade retention is very expensive → the money should be used for other things, e.g. to tutor students with problems more closely or to offer them prospects

Topic 15: A complaint

Listening text

Track 10

(Telefonklingeln)

MICHELLE: Hello, this is Sunshine Travels, Michelle O'Brian speaking, what can I do for you?

PAUL: Hello, this is Paul Smith speaking. We've just returned from a holiday in Sardinia and I would like to complain about our hotel, which we booked through your agency.

MICHELLE: Oh, I'm sorry to hear that. I'll write down your complaint in order to improve our service. So would you please give me your name once again?

PAUL: Of course, it's Paul Smith.

MICHELLE: Okay. And would you please also give me your address and telephone number, so we can contact you?

PAUL: Right, my address is 163 Rose Lane, Liverpool. The telephone number is 0151 496 0669.

MICHELLE: Let me repeat that to make sure I've got it down correctly. 163 Rose Lane, Liverpool. Telephone 0151 496 0669.

PAUL: That's it.

MICHELLE: Could I also have your e-mail address, please?

PAUL: That's paul.smith1965@yahoo.co.uk

MICHELLE: I'll repeat that, too. paul.smith1965@yahoo.co.uk. If you have your booking number, could you give that to me, too, please?

PAUL: Hold on a second … Here we go. It's 5634/88SAR.

MICHELLE: Okay, I've noted it all down. So, you said you were unhappy with your hotel. Where exactly were you staying?

PAUL: We stayed at the Palm Beach Hotel in Cagliari in Sardinia.

MICHELLE: What exactly were you unhappy about, sir?

PAUL *(gets more and more angry)*: In your brochure the hotel seemed very promising, but in reality it was quite intolerable. First, in the brochure it says that the hotel has been renovated, but really the work was still going on, so we were living on a building site, more like. There was noise all day. Second, it says in your brochure that the hotel's close to the town centre. I suppose three kilometres could be seen as quite close. However, there was no bus service, so we had to walk three kilometres to the town centre or take a taxi, which is quite expensive in Sardinia. And finally, the beach really is only 200 metres away from the hotel, but on the other side of a six-lane road. Can you imagine the noise on the beach? Altogether, it wasn't relaxing at all. Quite the contrary: it was noisy and stressful.

MICHELLE *(understanding)*: I'm really sorry to hear that, Mr Smith. So, to sum it up, you're complaining about the noise going on in the hotel and because of a big road close to the beach. And you're complaining that there was no bus service from the hotel to the town centre. Is that it?

PAUL: Yes, that about covers it. And we really want you to pay back at least half of the money we paid for the hotel.

MICHELLE: OK, I'll see what I can do for you. I've noted down all your complaints and I've got your address and everything. I'll contact the hotel manager to hear their version and then I'll get back to you. Of course, we're interested in satisfied clients and I'm sure we'll find a solution here.

PAUL *(demanding)*: I certainly do hope so. I won't just accept *any* solution. We really want part of our money back.

MICHELLE *(patient)*: Yes, as I said, we'll get back to you as soon as we've looked into the situation at Palm Beach Hotel. I'm truly grateful for your feedback, Mr Smith.

PAUL: All right. I expect to hear from you by the end of the week.

MICHELLE: You will, Mr Smith, you will. Goodbye and thank you.

PAUL: Goodbye.

48
a) Listing: **to start first / first, second, third / finally / last**
b) Addition: **also / moreover / in addition / besides / as well as / too**
c) Contrast: **although / whereas / however / even though**
d) Reason: **since / therefore / because of**
e) Conclusion: **to sum (it) up / in conclusion / to conclude / on the whole**

49 Someone is/was unhappy with his or her holiday, especially the hotel. He/She might complain about the noise, the food, the facilities, the service, etc.

50

Sunshine Travels

Client's name:	Paul Smith
Address:	163 Rose Lane, Liverpool
Telephone:	0151 496 0669
E-Mail:	paul.smith1965@yahoo.co.uk
Booking number:	5634/88SAR
Place of residence:	Palm Beach Hotel, Cagliari, Sardinia
Complaints:	1. noise all day
	2. no bus service from hotel to town;
	client had to walk or take an expensive taxi
	3. noisy beach on the other side of a
	six-lane road
Client's demand:	wants half/part of the money back that
	he paid for the hotel
Measures suggested:	contact hotel manager
	look at situation at the Palm Beach Hotel
	contact client by the end of the week

51
- The client's tone of voice at the beginning:
  - [x] polite
  - [ ] joking
  - [x] friendly
  - [ ] angry

- The assistant's tone of voice at the beginning:

  - [x] understanding
  - [x] polite
  - [ ] annoyed
  - [ ] unfriendly

Information we get at the beginning of the conversation:	Information about the client (name, address, etc.)
How does this match?	The client's tone of voice at the beginning is polite and friendly because he simply answers all the assistant's questions. / The client does not know the assistant and the assistant is not responsible for his complaints. It is the assistant's job to be polite to customers.

- The client's tone of voice towards the end:

  - [ ] understanding
  - [x] angry
  - [x] annoyed
  - [ ] joking

- The assistant's tone of voice towards the end:

  - [x] understanding
  - [x] polite
  - [ ] annoyed
  - [ ] unfriendly

Information we get at the end of the conversation:	The customer complains about his holidays.
How does this match?	The customer is angry about all the things that went wrong. / It is the assistants job to be polite towards customers.

Topic 16: An Inuit legend

Listening text 1

Track 11

A long, long time ago, Man was hunting for seals. It was really cold and he was looking for something to eat for Woman and Son. He had been on the prowl for quite some time and was beginning to worry that he might have to return without any food for the family.

He was about to give up, when he suddenly heard the grunts and rasps typical of seals. Man became excited and followed the sound. To his great joy he discovered a group of seals lying on the seashore. Man was all smiles now because he was sure to bring home enough meat to last for many days. Woman would prepare a great feast and all three would feed off it and not go hungry. Man was afraid because he knew that he had to be especially careful not to warn the seals of his presence. So he crept slowly and quietly toward the group of seals. However, the animals grew restless. So Man lay low for some time until the animals had calmed down again. Then he started to creep forward again. As he was hunting seals with a knife and not a harpoon, he had to get really close to a seal before he could attack it. On his side of the group, Man spotted a huge seal which would provide plenty of food. He was so happy. However, when he was almost close enough to use his knife, the seals started to bark and slipped away into the water before Man could strike. He was worried because his food was escaping. In his mind's eye, he could almost see the sad faces of Woman and Son when he returned home empty-handed.

But then he saw one last seal on the shore. It was smaller than the seal he had had his eye on at first, but it was also slower. Hope flared up inside Man again. Here was some food for Woman and Son after all. He slowly and carefully got closer to the seal, which didn't seem to notice him. But then, at the very last moment, it slipped away into the water and disappeared, and with it all hopes vanished, too.

Man rose to his feet. He felt really bad, but there was more to it than that. He was taken over by a strange and unknown emotion. He realized that water was trickling from his eyes, and when he touched his face, tasted the liquid, it tasted salty, like seawater. The strange emotion was completely new to him and he heard strange sounds. After only a few seconds did he understand that they were coming from his own body. He sank to the ground and could not stop making those sounds or keep the water from running from his eyes.

He did not know how long he had stayed on the seashore, when suddenly he realized Son and Woman were there. Son had heard Man's cries and had told Woman. Together they had quickly run to the seashore to find Man.

When they found him, however, they did not know what was wrong with him. Never before had they seen water running out of Man's eyes. They came closer and gave him surprised looks.

Man told them what had happened: how he had discovered the seals. How he had hoped for a good meal for all of them. He told them how he had crept closer and how high his hopes had been. And he also told them how first the big group and finally the smaller seal had escaped his knife. While Mother and Son were listening, salty drops began to trickle from their eyes, too. The trickle turned into a stream of tears and Woman and Son were crying with Man. Thus, people learned to weep.

Listening text 2

Track 12

a) A long, long time ago, Man was hunting for seals. It was really cold and he was looking for something to eat for Woman and Son. He had been on the prowl for quite some time and was beginning to worry that he might have to return without any food for the family.

b) He was about to give up, when he suddenly heard the grunts and rasps typical of seals. Man became excited and followed the sound.

c) He was worried because his food was escaping. In his mind's eye, he could almost see the sad faces of Woman and Son when he returned home empty-handed. But then he saw one last seal on the shore. It was smaller than the seal he had had his eye on at first, but it was also slower. Hope flared up inside Man again. Here was some food for Woman and Son after all.

d) While Mother and Son were listening, salty drops began to trickle from their eyes, too. The trickle turned into a stream of tears and Woman and Son were crying with Man. Thus, people learned to weep.

52 a) The Inuit People …

- ☐ live in Australia.
- ☑ live on the North American continent.
- ☐ are also called Indians.
- ☑ are sometimes called Eskimos.

b) Legends …

- ☑ are stories.
- ☑ sometimes explain how the natural world works.
- ☑ tell of events that are said to have happened a long time ago.
- ☑ often have a message.

53

Who?	Man, seals, Woman, Son
Where?	on a seashore
When?	a long, long time ago
What?	Man wants to hunt for food, tries to catch seals, is not successful, seals escape, starts to cry (Woman and Son find him, don't recognise tears, hear Man's story, start to cry, too)
Why?	Man wants to hunt because family is hungry; he feels really bad because there is no food for his family
Myth?	tears, people learn to cry/weep

54 a) to be on the prowl: **to move quietly and carefully in order not to be heard or seen** *(auf der Jagd nach etwas sein)*

b) grunts and rasps: **sounds made by seals** *(Grunzen und Krächzen)*

c) to flare up (hope): **to suddenly be hopeful again** *(aufkeimen)*

d) to trickle: **to flow slowly in a thin line** *(tropfen, rinnen)*

55

Emotions	Reasons
worried	he worries that he will have to return to his family without food
excited	he hears sounds typically made by seals
happy	he discovers a group of seals on the seashore
afraid	the animals escape
sad	the last seal disappears and he knows that there is no food now for him and his family

56 *(Lösungsvorschlag)*

The characters are not given any names because the story is not about one particular man and his wife and son but about mankind *(die Menschheit)* in general. The focus of the story is not on the characters themselves, but on how mankind learned to weep.

Topic 17: Strategien zum Hörverstehen

57 *(Lösungsvorschlag)*

Listening-Strategies
Vor dem Hören: ➡ Vermutungen über den Text anstellen (mit Hilfe von Bildern, Überschrift, Aufgaben und Textsorte) (S. 36) ➡ Vorwissen zum Thema aktivieren (S. 36) ➡ Wortschatz zum Thema aktivieren (S. 36) ➡ Schlüsselwörter in der Aufgabenstellung markieren (S. 41) ➡ Synonyme/Umschreibungen zu den Schlüsselwörtern finden (S. 41)
Während des Hörens: ➡ Notizen machen: W-Fragen (S. 41) ➡ Notizen machen: Substantive, Verben, Namen, Zahlen (S. 43) ➡ Auf Signalwörter achten (S. 48) ➡ Gehörtes interpretieren (S. 50)
Wenn ich Wörter nicht verstehe: ➡ aus dem Zusammenhang erschließen (S. 45)
Nach dem (ersten) Hören: ➡ fehlende Lösungen markieren (S. 38) ➡ Aufgaben markieren, die überprüft werden müssen (S. 38)

Words and spelling

Topic 18: Peers and friends

Listening text: vgl. Aufgabe

58 Peter's highly unusual behaviour annoyed his classmates intensely. He used to shout really loudly whenever he said something. And what he said was usually downright stupid, too. We all criticised him strongly and some students even started bullying him, but still he didn't change his behaviour. Today, I strongly believe that he just couldn't help it and I am deeply sorry for making his life at school utterly miserable.

Track 13

highly unusual – (to) annoy sb intensely – really loud(ly) – downright stupid – (to) criticize sb strongly / (to) strongly believe – (to) (be) deeply sorry – (to make sb's life) utterly miserable

59
a) a casual acquaintance ≠ **a close friend**
b) to form a friendship ≠ **to break up a friendship**
c) a fair-weather friend ≠ **a true friend**
d) to lose contact with sb ≠ **to keep in touch with sb**

The two expressions not needed are …
- **a circle of friends**
- **to make friends with sb**

60

to break up a friendship	*eine Freundschaft beenden*
a casual acquaintance	*ein*e flüchtige*r Bekannte*r*
d circle of friends	*mein Freundeskreis*
a close friend	*ein*e enge*r Freund*in*
a fair-weather friend	*ein*e Schön-Wetter-Freund*in*
to form a friendship	*Freundschaft schließen*
to keep in touch with sb	*in Kontakt bleiben*
to lose contact with sb	*Kontakt verlieren*
to make friends with sb	*Freundschaft schließen, sich anfreunden*

61 *(Lösungsvorschlag)*
When I changed from primary to secondary school I soon **lost contact with** most of my former friends. Of course, I **kept in touch with** those boys and girls who changed to the same school, and **I made friends with** quite a few new people then. After some weeks in our new class, we went on a class trip together and that helped our friendship to grow. Over time, however, some **friendships broke up** and others were newly **formed**. I also found out that not all the people in **my circle of friends** were really **true friends**. Two or three proved to be mere **fair-weather friends** who I couldn't count on in times of trouble.

Topic 19: Describing characters

62

V	R	T	C	L	E	V	E	R	U	I	P	D	E	X
S	E	N	S	I	T	I	V	E	E	R	B	I	M	E
O	L	K	S	D	F	L	D	L	Y	R	C	N	K	B
A	I	S	R	T	W	U	N	D	I	N	K	G	D	E
C	K	P	E	S	S	I	M	I	S	T	I	C	S	K
Z	E	O	N	V	R	B	T	H	A	P	P	Y	X	I
F	A	O	G	C	U	K	A	B	K	E	L	W	E	N
R	B	R	O	A	I	N	S	E	K	U	R	E	S	D
I	L	A	N	I	U	E	W	T	I	O	U	S	E	T
E	R	A	E	B	O	R	I	N	G	K	O	S	K	L
N	J	N	T	L	C	V	U	L	I	B	C	N	B	S
D	D	G	I	L	S	O	R	E	L	I	A	B	L	E
L	B	R	H	O	P	U	G	L	Y	M	Z	N	F	G
Y	R	Y	K	D	M	S	A	R	Z	O	B	E	I	N
A	B	S	U	L	R	V	S	J	E	K	T	K	I	L

positive trait	negative trait
sensitive	nervous
clever	angry
friendly	boring
kind	poor
reliable	ugly
happy	pessimistic

63

English		German	
positive trait	**negative trait**	***positive Eigenschaft***	***negative Eigenschaft***
sensitive	insensitive	*sensibel, einfühlsam*	*gefühllos, taktlos*
relaxed	nervous	*entspannt*	*nervös*
calm	angry	*ruhig, gelassen*	*wütend*
interesting	boring	*interessant*	*langweilig*
clever	stupid	*klug*	*dumm*
friendly	unfriendly	*freundlich*	*unfreundlich*
kind	cruel	*nett, liebenswürdig*	*gemein, grausam*
reliable	unreliable	*zuverlässig*	*unzuverlässig*
optimistic	pessimistic	*optimistisch, zuversichtlich*	*pessimistisch*
rich	poor	*reich*	*arm*
pretty	ugly	*schön, hübsch*	*häßlich*
happy	sad	*glücklich*	*traurig*

64 a) Sam always tells the same stories and he only ever wants to talk about football. He is really a very **boring** person to talk to.

b) I can't believe how **stupid** she is. She doesn't understand the simplest things and she will do anything you tell her to do without thinking.

c) Terry really believes that he will pass his exam. He hasn't revised at all and he's missed quite a few lessons, but he is still very **optimistic** that he will do just fine.

d) Sally wanted to pick me up for the party at 7 pm. We had to be at Maria's at 7.30 but at 7.20 she still hadn't arrived. When I called her, she was still getting dressed. I just can't believe how **unreliable** she is.

e) Our teacher got really mad at us when he realized that none of us had done our homework. I don't think I've ever seen him so **angry**. He shouted at us for about 5 minutes.

f) Mr Gonzalez can't stand cats. Whenever he can, he throws stones at them. He told his neighbour he would kill their cat if it ever came into their garden again. He is really a very **cruel** man.

65 *(Lösungsvorschlag)*
I'm not quite sure how other people see me, but I think I'm a rather **friendly** person. I always greet people in the street and I also help others if I can. I'm definitely **reliable**. If I make a promise, I'll be sure to keep it. That's because I cannot stand people who are **unreliable** myself. If someone offers me a ride, for example, but doesn't show up, that really makes me **angry**. But usually I'm **calm**. It really takes a lot to make me scream and shout. Mostly, when I'm with my friends, I feel really **happy**. Sometimes I just can't stop laughing. My friends often tell me that I'm a very **optimistic** person. I rarely worry but mostly believe that everything will turn out fine.

Topic 20: The fence

66

verb	noun(s)	adjective(s)	*Wortfeld*
–	**racism, racist**	racist	*Rassismus*
(to) immigrate to	**immigrant, immigration**	**immigrated**	**Einwanderung**
(to) discriminate against	**discrimination**	**discriminated (against)**	**Diskriminierung**
(to) hope	hope	**hopeful, hopeless**	**Hoffnung**
(to) differ	difference	**different**	**Unterschied**
–	**majority**	major	**Mehrheit**
–	**minority**	minor	*Minderheit*
–	**nation, nationality**	national	**Nation, (Herkunfts)land**
(to) smuggle	smuggling, **smuggler**	–	**Schmuggel**

67 a) There are many reasons **for** people to leave their home country. Some leave because they live **in** poverty and they hope **for** a better future in a different country. Others suffer **from** discrimination, and some people even fear **for** their lives.

Reasons for leaving:

- **weil sie in Armut leben**
- **weil sie auf eine bessere Zukunft hoffen**
- **weil sie unter Diskriminierung leiden**
- **weil sie um ihr Leben fürchten**

b)

A	B	C	D	E
3	5	2	4	1

c)

A	B	C	D	E
4	2	1	5	3

68 INTERVIEWER: Good morning, Mrs Ramirez. Thank you for your time and for sharing your story with us. Why don't you start by telling us what brought you to San Diego.

MRS RAMIREZ: I was born in a little village in Mexico. We lived in poverty there. Our situation was really desperate because in Mexico there is a lot of crime and we often feared for **our lives**. Our children were of course much younger then. We wanted a better future for them. That's why we decided to leave Mexico.

INTERVIEWER: But it isn't easy to cross the US-Mexico border – not with the tight controls and the fence.

MRS RAMIREZ: Yes, that was the hardest part. We tried to cross **the border** illegally a few times. But we were always caught by the border patrol and sent back. Finally we decided to pay a **smuggler** to take us over the border. In the dead of night we walked to the fence and he showed us a spot where to **climb** the fence. My family was lucky. We made it and were hidden on the American side when the border control came. But ten people in our group were caught that night.

INTERVIEWER: What is life like here in San Diego?

MRS RAMIREZ: Now we are really happy. Two years ago we finally became US Americans but it took a lot to get there. First we took on any kind of farm work we could get. It was frustrating because my husband is a mechanic and I am a nurse, but we could only find **unskilled** work. And we were always afraid of being discovered and sent back to Mexico.

INTERVIEWER: What was it like for your children?

MRS RAMIREZ: They went to school here, so they had to **get along / grow up** in two cultures. They were often **discriminated** against because their parents are **immigrants**. They often cried at home and didn't want to return to school. But we explained how important education is. As a result they have grown up **bilingually**, which is an important advantage for them because it will help them to find a job.

INTERVIEWER: Does that mean you're happy with your decision to leave your home country?

MRS RAMIREZ: Absolutely. Of course, I do miss my home and my family, but we've built a good life for ourselves here. The first couple of years were really hard, though. But now I can even send some money to my family, back in Mexico from time to time. Sometimes we still have to **face / fight** discrimination but in our neighbourhood the **majority** of the people are Hispanics, so it feels a bit like home.

INTERVIEWER: Thank you for your time, Mrs Ramirez.

Topic 21: Feelings and emotions

69 a) *(Lösungsvorschlag)*

surprised / upset / worried / annoyed

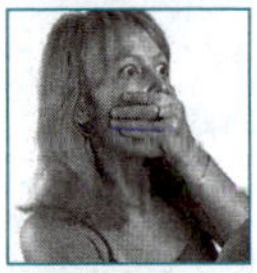

shocked / horrified / afraid / scared

enthusiastic / happy / proud / joyful

unhappy / sad / puzzled / disappointed

annoyed / angry / furious / mad

b)

70

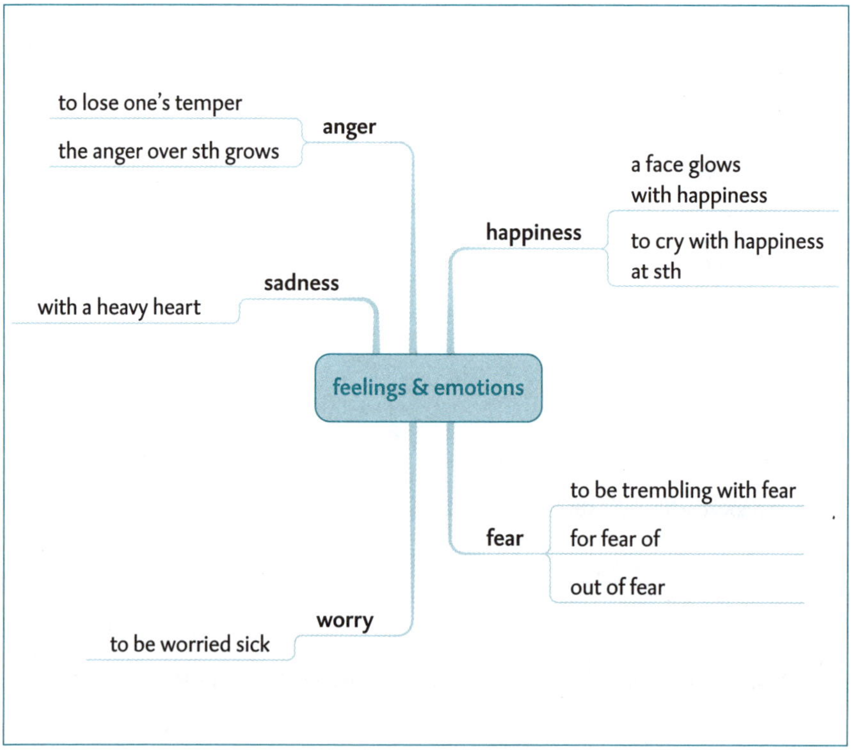

71

disappointment	dissatisfied with sb/sth deeply disappointed with sb upset about
embarrassment	embarrassed at/by ashamed of
jealousy	madly jealous of to go green with envy
regret	sorry about sth/for sb to my regret
excitement	excited about nervous about enthusiastic about

72 a) She is **terribly frightened** of spiders.
b) He is **extremely pleased** that he still got tickets for the concert.
c) I'm **really sad** that you're leaving.
d) They are **deeply concerned** about their son.
e) They are **terribly angry** at their teacher.

73 a) Mary has just got the results of her exams and now her face is **glowing** with happiness. Last night she was worried **sick** for fear of the results but at the moment she is **extremely** pleased with herself. She could easily **cry** with happiness.
b) When Sue saw her boyfriend with her best friend she was **madly** jealous. She was too **deeply** disappointed with both of them to say anything. But on her way home her anger **grew** and she finally **lost** her temper and called her boyfriend.
c) To my great **regret** my favourite band split up. Whenever I listen to their last CD, I do so with a **heavy** heart. I'm **deeply** depressed by their decision and could go **green** with envy because my sister went to their last concert.

Topic 22: US history

74 a) independence
b) **explorer**
c) **settlers**
d) **pilgrims**
e) **disease**
f) **(to) survive**
g) **harvest**
h) **colony**
i) **traditions**
j) **(to) found**

75 b) independence → to declare, to win, ~~difficult~~, hard-won
- **We hereby declare independence!**
- **The former colonies won independence.**
- **It was a really hard-won independence.**

c) disease → to catch, to spread, to treat, ~~to give~~
- **The settlers spread disease(s) among the Native Americans.**
- **The Native Americans caught these new diseases.**
- **Unfortunately, they had no way to treat these diseases.**

d) survive → ~~poorly~~, hardly, to struggle, to manage
- **The settlers hardly survived the first winter.**
- **They struggled to survive in the new colony.**
- **They managed to survive with the help of the Native Americans.**

e) colony → to found, small, overseas, ~~to take~~
- **The settlers founded a new colony.**
- **Delaware was only a small colony.**
- **First, America was a British overseas colony.**

76 In 1620 the first **settlers** from Europe **founded** a colony they called Plymouth. Unfortunately, they spread **diseases** which the Native Americans weren't able to **treat**. In autumn, the **settlers** only brought in a poor **harvest** and many died of hunger and cold during the first winter.
Others managed to **survive**. They fought with the Native Americans over the land and later against the British for **independence**. Today, the Native Americans are trying to keep their centuries-old **traditions** alive.

Topic 23: British and American English

77 a)

Track 14

British English	American English
centre	center
kilometre	kilometer
litre	liter
theatre	theater

b)

British English	American English
colour	color
neighbour	neighbor
harbour	harbor

c)

British English	American English
to organise	to organize
to analyse	**to analyze**
to apologise	**to apologize**
to recognise	**to recognize**

d)

British English	American English
defence	defense
pretence	**pretense**
licence	**license**

e)

British English	American English
to marvel, marvelled	to marvel, marveled
to travel, travelled, travelling	**to travel, traveled, traveling**

78 Track 15

a) This morning there was a message on the **notice board** announcing a **sports day** for next Friday. I guess I'll play **football** then.

b) When I entered the building, I heard the **caretaker** talking to the **headmaster/head teacher**. He complained that the students left too much **rubbish** on the floor and did not use the **bins/dustbins/rubbish bins**.

c) Just look at my **timetable**. Each day starts with **maths**. How horrible! I need a **holiday** already!

d) My cousin used to have very bad **marks/grades**. Then he changed to a very expensive **public school** and this **year** he is doing much better.

e) We should have taken the **Tube/underground** to go **to the city centre**.

f) The traffic on the **motorway** is very heavy again. I wish I had a **motorbike**. I'd be much quicker then.

g) I'm hungry. Can't we stop here for some **chips**?

h) **Mum**, can we buy some **crisps** before we go to the **cinema**?

79

Track 16

1

a) British English ☐
b) American English ☑

2

a) British English ☑
b) American English ☐

3

a) British English ☐
b) American English ☑

4

a) British English ☑
b) American English ☐

5

a) British English ☑
b) American English ☐

6

a) British English ☐
b) American English ☑

Topic 24: Strategien zum Wortschatz

80 *(Lösungsvorschlag)*

Learning-Strategies
Vokabeln lernen: ➡ jeden Tag 5-10 Minuten (S. 57) ➡ mündlich und schriftlich üben ➡ Vokabelkasten oder -heft ➡ Lernsoftware ➡ keine isolierten Wörter, sondern Kollokationen lernen (S. 58) ➡ Präpositionen mitlernen (S. 66) ➡ Wörter umwälzen (S. 59)
Wortschatz erweitern: ➡ Synonyme und Antonyme sammeln (S. 59) ➡ Bedeutung von Vor- und Nachsilben kennen und nutzen (S. 62) ➡ mit Wortfamilien arbeiten (S. 65)
Rechtschreibregeln: ➡ Endsilbe -ful mit einem „l", z.B. hopeful (S. 72) ➡ British vs. American English (S. 77/78) –re → –er –our → –or –ise → –ize –ence → -ense –ll– → -l-

Mediation

Topic 25: Going shopping

81
- Ziel/Absicht: **Verständnisprobleme beheben, Inhalt der Schilder erklären**
- Für wen: **eine Cousine aus Amerika**
- Wortwahl: **umgangssprachlich, neutral**

82 b) Here you can collect points when you pay. If you have a Shopping Card, you collect points for everything you buy. Today and tomorrow they will give you five times the normal number of points/ they'll multiply the points by five.

c) People under 18 are not allowed to go in there. / If you want to go in there, you need to be 18 at least.

d) If you want to buy cigarettes or alcohol you need to show an official document, such as your identity card, so that they can check your age, because it is hard to say how old someone is by looking at them. (In Germany you have to be 18 to buy cigarettes and 16 or 18 to buy alcohol. It depends on what kind of alcohol you want to buy.)

e) It is a special offer at weekends. You get one loaf of bread and ten rolls/ buns for € 4.99.

Topic 26: Taking part in an exchange

Track 17

Listening Text

DIREKTOR: Liebe Schülerinnen, liebe Schüler, liebe Kolleginnen und Kollegen, ich freue mich sehr, dass wir in dieser Woche erneut Freunde unserer englischen Partnerschule zu Gast haben. Dieser Austausch besteht bereits seit zehn Jahren und in dieser Zeit haben fast 300 englische Schülerinnen und Schüler unsere Schule besucht und ein paar Tage mit uns verbracht, um einen Einblick in das deutsche Schulsystem zu bekommen und vor allem um Freundschaften quer über den Kanal zu schließen.

Ich danke allen beteiligten Kolleginnen und Kollegen, vor allem Keira Smith, die diesen Austausch vor zehn Jahren ins Leben gerufen hat und ihn seither aufrechterhält. Liebe Keira, ohne dich wären wir heute alle nicht

hier. *(Applaus)* Als Zeichen des Dankes und unserer Verbundenheit haben wir ein T-Shirt mit den Bildern und Logos unserer Schule für dich anfertigen lassen. Auf der Rückseite sind sehr viele Unterschriften von Schülerinnen und Schülern, die bislang an dem Austausch teilgenommen haben. *(Applaus)*
Liebe Schülerinnen und Schüler, wie in den letzten Jahren, werdet ihr in dieser Woche ein interessantes Programm erleben. Ihr werdet einen Tag am Unterricht teilnehmen, eine Führung durch unsere Stadt aber auch durch Köln machen. Ihr werdet euch sportlich betätigen und sicherlich viele interessante Erfahrungen in euren Gastfamilien machen. Ihr alle tragt dazu bei, die europäische Idee mit Leben zu füllen und dafür danke ich euch ganz herzlich. Seid also herzlich willkommen in unserer Schule, unserer Stadt und in unserem Land und nehmt viele positive Eindrücke mit zurück nach England. *(Applaus)*

83 a)
- Ziel: **Verständnisprobleme beheben, Informationen einer deutschsprachigen Rede auf Englisch zusammenfassen**
- Für wen: **Tanita; englische Austauschschülerin**
- Wortwahl: **umgangssprachlich, neutral**

b) TANITA: What does he say? There are 300 pupils here? That's not true.

YOU: **No, I'm afraid you got that wrong. He said that the partnership between our schools has existed for ten years now and that almost 300 pupils have taken part in the exchange in those years.**

TANITA: And what does he say about Mrs Smith?

YOU: **He thanked Mrs Smith for starting the exchange ten years ago and for keeping it alive. He says that it is because of her that we are all standing here today.**

TANITA: And what about the T-shirt that she got? I could see the pictures on the front and lots of names on the back. Who signed it?

YOU: **On the back there are lots of names of the German pupils who took part in the exchange in the last ten years.**

TANITA: I think I understood what he said about the programme, but then at the end he said what we should take home. Will we get T-shirts too?

YOU: **No, I'm sorry, there's no T-shirt for you. He hopes that you will take home a lot of positive impressions/memories from our school, our town and our country.**

84 BROTHER: *Schau mal, Tanita, das bin ich am ersten Schultag. Da war ich sehr nervös, aber alle waren sehr nett, vor allem meine Lehrerin.*

YOU: He says that on this picture you can see him on his first day at school. **He was very nervous but everyone was very nice, especially his teacher.**

TANITA: The picture looks really nice, but what is that thing you're holding?

YOU: **Sie findet das Bild sehr schön, aber sie weiß nicht, was du da in der Hand hältst.**

BROTHER: *Aber das ist doch meine Schultüte. Anscheinend weiß Sie nicht, was das ist. Erklär es ihr doch mal.*

YOU: **That's called a "Schultüte" in Germany. It's a special present that children get on their first day at school. Usually it's quite big and the new pupils carry it around at school and have their photo taken with it. It's made of card.**

TANITA: OK. I've never heard of that. Was there anything inside?

YOU: **Sie hat noch nie davon gehört. Den Brauch gibt es wohl in Großbritannien nicht. Sie fragt, ob was drin war.**

BROTHER: *Ja, es waren viele Süßigkeiten, Farbstifte und ein Stundenplan drin. Jetzt muss ich aber meine Hausaufgaben machen. Tschüß, Tanita.*

YOU: **There were a lot of sweets inside the "Schultüte" and also some felt tip pens and pencil crayons and a timetable. He says he has to do his homework now and says goodbye.**

TANITA: Yeah. Bye.

Topic 27: A visit to Chicago

85 a) MUM: „Kannst du bitte auch fragen, ob es ein Tagesticket für Bus und Bahn gibt und wie viel das kostet?"

Can you tell me if there is a day ticket for public transport, please?
And can you also tell me how much that costs?

MUM: „Mich interessiert noch, wo die nächste U-Bahn-Station ist. Kann man dort dann Tickets kaufen oder ist das im Hotel möglich?"

Where is the next/nearest subway station?
Can we buy tickets there or can we do that at the hotel?

MUM: „Und frag bitte noch, was sie Touristen als Hauptattraktion empfehlen."

Which sights do you recommend?/
Which sights do you think we should see?

MUM: „Außerdem möchte ich wissen, wie das Wetter nächste Woche in Chicago wird und ob es dort oft regnet."

What will the weather be like next week?
Does it rain a lot in Chicago?

b) *(Lösungsvorschlag)*

Zunächst einmal sagen sie, dass wir einen Stadtplan und einen Plan der öffentlichen Verkehrsmittel an der Rezeption im Hotel bekommen. Sie empfehlen uns außerdem gleich ein 3-Tagesticket zu erwerben. Das kostet $ 20 und wir können es an der nächstgelegenen Bahnstation kaufen, die sich 300 Yards (also knapp 300 Meter) die Straße runter befindet.

Als eine der Hauptattraktionen empfehlen sie eine spezielle Bootstour. Da bekommen wir einen guten ersten Eindruck von der Stadt und erfahren viel über die Gebäude entlang des Flusses und die Stadtgeschichte.

Das Wetter soll nächste Woche schön werden, aber der Wetterbericht hält leichten Regen am Ende der Woche für wahrscheinlich. Das kann in dieser Jahreszeit leider immer vorkommen.

86 a) *Markierungen im Text siehe unten:*

FIRE ACTION!!!

IF YOU DISCOVER A FIRE

1. *Operate the nearest fire alarm. The emergency plan will tell you where to find it.*
2. *Dial 911 to call the fire department. Tell them who you are, what has happened and where you are. Don't hang up before being told to do so.*
3. *If possible, tackle the fire using the appliances provided. The emergency plan will tell you where the fire extinguishers are. Be careful not to endanger yourself or others when doing so.*

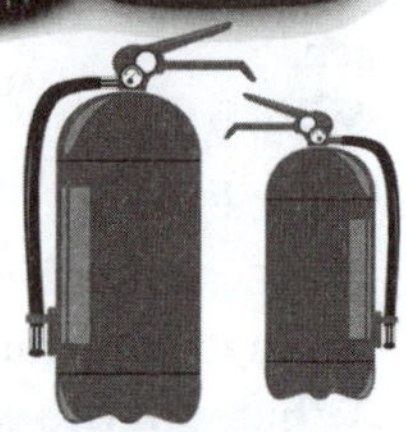

IF YOU HEAR THE FIRE ALARM

4. *Leave the building by the nearest available exit. Follow the green signs.*
5. *If possible, help others who need assistance.*
6. *Use the stairs. Do not use the lift!*
7. *Close all doors behind you.*
8. *Report to the person in charge of the assembly point.*

CAUTION

9. *If smoke is heavy in the corridors, it may be safer to stay in your room. Close the door and place a wet towel at the base of the door. A rescue team will come in less than 5 minutes.*

ABOVE ALL: REMAIN CALM

b) *(Lösungsvorschlag)*
Schau mal, hier ist ein Infoblatt, wie wir uns bei einem Brand verhalten müssen. Also, wenn wir ein Feuer bemerken, müssen wir natürlich Alarm auslösen. Auf dem Notfallplan können wir nachsehen, wo der nächste Alarmknopf ist. Dann rufen wir die Feuerwehr. Hier in den USA ist die Notrufnummer die 911.
Wenn es nicht zu gefährlich ist, kann man auch versuchen, den Brand zu löschen. Auf dem Notfallplan sind die Feuerlöscher eingezeichnet. Sollte es einen Feueralarm geben, können wir an den grünen Schildern den schnellsten Weg aus dem Gebäude erkennen. Denen folgen wir dann einfach, wobei wir alle Türen hinter uns schließen sollen. Draußen gibt es dann einen Sammelpunkt und dort müssen wir uns melden. Den Aufzug dürfen wir auf keinen Fall benutzen.
Hier, das ist auch noch wichtig: Wenn der Rauch im Flur zu stark ist, bleiben wir besser im Zimmer. Dann sollen wir ein nasses Handtuch vor den Türspalt legen und warten. Ein Rettungsteam ist spätestens nach fünf Minuten da. Das ist doch beruhigend zu wissen.
Und vor allem sollen wir Ruhe bewahren. Jetzt sind wir doch gut informiert und du musst dir keine Gedanken mehr machen.

Topic 28: Camp Cooper

87 a) **tuition** [tjuːˈɪʃn; US auch tʊ-] s
n **1.** *(besonders Einzel-, Privat)* **Unterricht** *m*
2. *besonders* US
a) (SCHULE) **Schulgeld** *n*
b) (UNIV) **Studiengebühren** *pl*

b) **ratio** [ˈreɪʃɪəʊ; US auch -ʃəʊ] pl -os s
n **1.** (MATH) *etc* **Verhältnis** *n*
2. (MATH) **Quotient** *m*
3. (WIRTSCH) **Wertverhältnis** *n* **zwischen Gold und Silber**
4. (TECH) **Übersetzungsverhältnis** *n (eines Getriebes)*

c) **suit** [suːt; BE auch sjuːt]
v **1.** **passen**
2. *(Kleider, Farben etc.)* **stehen**
3. *besonders* BE *(gut tun)* **bekommen** *(meist verneinte Sätze)*

d) **exceptional** [ikˈsepʃənl]
adj **1.** **hervorragend**
2. **auffällig**
3. **ungewöhnlich**

e) **encourage** [inˈkʌridʒ; US -ˈɜːr-]

v **1.** *(to encourage sth)* **fördern**
2. *(to encourage sb)* **ermutigen**
3. (SPORT) **anfeuern**

f) **develop** [diˈveləp]

v **1. entstehen**
2. *sich (aus etw) (zu etw)* **entwickeln**
3. *(Fehler etc.)* **auftreten**

g) **confidence** [ˈkɒnfɪdəns; US ˈkɑːn-]

n **1. Zuversicht**
2. Vertrauen
3. Selbstbewusstsein

h) **recommend** [rekəˈmend]

v **1. (weiter)empfehlen**
2. *(jmd für etw)* **vorschlagen** *(z. B. Beförderung)*
3. befürworten

88 *(Lösungsvorschlag)*
Ich habe hier eine interessante Seite über das Camp Cooper gefunden. Das Camp ist in Schottland und ist für Kinder und Jugendliche zwischen 7 und 17 Jahren aus Großbritannien und anderen Ländern. Man kann dort 2, 4 oder 6 Wochen bleiben.
Es werden jede Menge Aktivitäten angeboten, z. B. Sport, Kunst, Theater, Tanz, Musik, Einblicke in die Filmproduktion und Naturabenteuer, aber auch Sprachkurse.
Abends gibt es Talent Shows, Musik Festivals, Hawaiianische Luaus, Lagerfeuer und irgendwas, das „Colour Competitions", also „Farbwettbewerbe", genannt wird.
Es wird dort viel Wert darauf gelegt, dass man sowohl Selbstständigkeit, als auch Selbstbewusstsein und Führungsqualitäten entwickelt. Außerdem ist den Veranstaltern wichtig, dass man Freundschaften schließt, Kreativität entwickelt, wichtige Fertigkeiten lernt und Spaß hat.
Eltern sind offensichtlich sehr begeistert von dem Camp, denn sie haben es mit 9,5 von 10 Punkten bewertet und würden es weiterempfehlen.

89
1. How many English lessons can I have/take per week? / How many English lessons are given/taught every/each week?
2. How long does one lesson last? / How long is one lesson?
3. How many students/pupils are (there) in one class?
4. Are there any extra costs for day trips, activities and so on? / Do day trips, activities, etc. cost extra? / Do I have to pay for day trips or special activities? / Are day trips and special activities included in the price?
5. Where are the day trips to? / Where do we go to on day trips?

6. What is the "colour competition" you mention on your website? / Could you explain what a "colour competition" is? Does it have anything to do with paintball?
7. How many teenagers are there/sleep in one tent?
8. Is it possible to return home without my parents? / Do my parents have to pick me up or can I go home alone/on my own? How?

90 **Listening Text**

Track 18

Ian: Hello, Camp Cooper, this is Ian MacNicol speaking. How may I help you?

Mia: Hello, this is Mia from Germany speaking. I'm thinking of joining Camp Cooper next summer and I'd like to get some more information for my parents. Could you answer some questions for me, please?

Ian: Of course, just fire away.

Mia: Okay. I'd like to improve my English, so I'm wondering how many English lessons I could get.

Ian: You can get up to ten lessons a week. So it depends on how long you want to stay with us. You can stay here two, four or six weeks. All in all you could have up to 60 lessons if you wanted to.

Mia: I'd probably stay for two weeks. So that's twenty lessons then. How long does one lesson last?

Ian: Each lesson lasts 50 minutes. There are small classes of no more than 15 pupils and we have highly qualified teachers, so you learn a lot. However, if you really do ten lessons per week, you won't be able to join our other great activities, such as mountain biking or outdoor adventures.

Mia: I see. I need to discuss that with my parents, I'm afraid. Talking of activities – are there any extra fees for those activities?

Ian: No, of course not. You pay € 1,400 for two weeks and that covers everything – except your journey to Scotland, of course. We even pick you up at the airport or train station without charging any fees. All day trips and activities, food and so on are included.

Mia: Great. Where do the day trips go to, by the way?

Ian: The camp is located in Crieff, which is right in the middle of Scotland's amazing countryside and woodlands. But we're also close to Edinburgh and Glasgow. We'll visit both cities at weekends so you can experience our culture. We'll visit Edinburgh Castle together, for example. You'll also have some free time there to explore the cities on your own.

Mia: OK. On your website I read something about a "colour competition". What's that? It sounds like "paintball shooting".

IAN: *(laughs)* Oh, right. Yeah, some parents get confused by that. Well, it's actually quite harmless. As I said before, we want you to experience Scottish culture. So we organise one day with a lot of typical games. We divide campers and staff into two teams, the Celts and the Vikings, and you get dressed in different colours. You compete against each other in different games. It's a lot of fun really and your parents don't need to worry. It isn't about paintball shooting or anything like that.

MIA: All right – they'll be relieved. Well, let me see, what else is on my list ... Right, we're almost done. I was wondering how many campers stay in one tent.

IAN: *(confused)* Tents? What do you mean?

MIA: *(confused)* Well, it is a camp, isn't it? So I guess we sleep in tents, don't we?

IAN: *(laughs)* Oh, I see. No, we don't have tents – we have cabins. You'll be quite comfortable – you'll sleep in real beds. There are four to six campers in one room and we arrange them according to gender and age but we mix nationalities. If you want to share a room with a friend, you can do so.

MIA: That's great. I really prefer sleeping in a cabin to sleeping in a tent ... I've got one last question. My parents will take me to the camp but they won't be able to pick me up again. Can I return home on my own?

IAN: Of course you can. We encourage independence a lot. We'll either take you to the airport or the train station, depending on how you travel home. We'll make sure that you get onto your train or to the boarding gate at the airport safely. Again, your parents can really be reassured. Your safety is very important to us.

MIA: They'll be glad to hear that, I'm sure. Thanks a lot for your time. You've really helped me an awful lot.

IAN: You're welcome, Mia. I'm looking forward to meeting you at Camp Cooper then. Bye.

MIA: Bye.

a) *(Lösungsvorschlag) Die Notizen in Klammern wurden nicht ausdrücklich erfragt, können dir aber helfen, deine Eltern in einem Gespräch zu überzeugen, dich an dem Camp teilnehmen zu lassen. Es wäre auch möglich, hier Notizen in deutscher Sprache anzufertigen.*

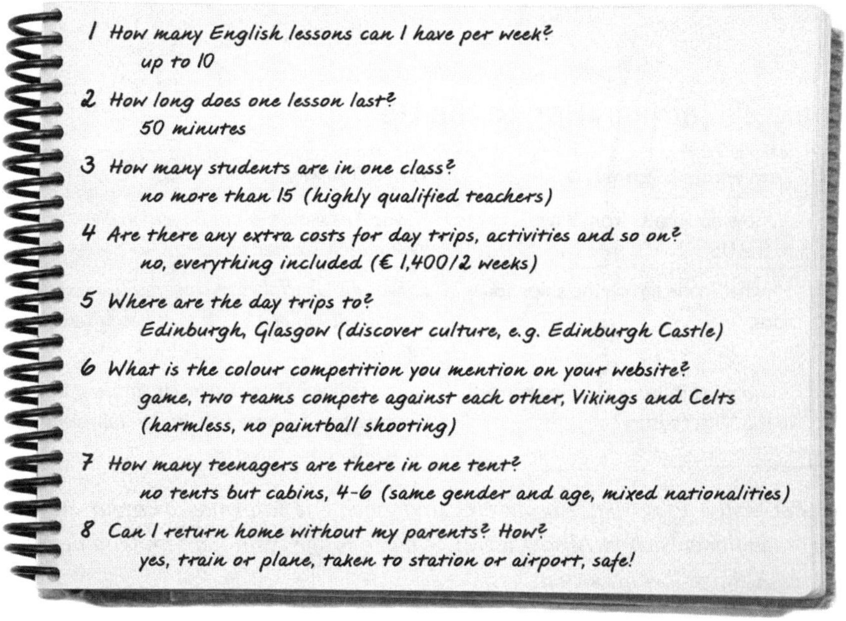

1 How many English lessons can I have per week?
up to 10

2 How long does one lesson last?
50 minutes

3 How many students are in one class?
no more than 15 (highly qualified teachers)

4 Are there any extra costs for day trips, activities and so on?
no, everything included (€ 1,400/2 weeks)

5 Where are the day trips to?
Edinburgh, Glasgow (discover culture, e.g. Edinburgh Castle)

6 What is the colour competition you mention on your website?
game, two teams compete against each other, Vikings and Celts (harmless, no paintball shooting)

7 How many teenagers are there in one tent?
no tents but cabins, 4–6 (same gender and age, mixed nationalities)

8 Can I return home without my parents? How?
yes, train or plane, taken to station or airport, safe!

b) *(Lösungsvorschlag)* Ich habe jetzt mit dem Camp telefoniert und die Informationen erhalten. Also, ich kann bis zu 10 Stunden Englischunterricht pro Woche bekommen. Die Stunden dauern jeweils 50 Minuten und es sind maximal 15 Schüler und Schülerinnen in einer Klasse. (Außerdem sind die Lehrer hoch qualifiziert und ich kann dort sicher viel lernen.)
(Das Camp kostet 1 400 Euro für zwei Wochen.) Zusätzliche Kosten fallen nicht an. Die Tagesausflüge gehen nach Edinburgh und Glasgow. (Sie legen Wert darauf, dass wir die schottische Kultur kennenlernen, und wir besichtigen das Edinburgh Castle/die Burg von Edinburgh.)
Der Farbwettkampf ist ganz harmlos. (Das hat gar nichts mit Paintball zu tun.) Zwei Teams, die Wikinger und die Kelten, treten in Spielen gegeneinander an.
Zelte gibt es dort gar nicht, wir wohnen in Hütten. Es sind immer 4–6 Personen in einem Zimmer. (Die Zimmer werden nach Geschlecht und Alter belegt, aber die Nationalitäten werden gemischt.)

Die Rückkehr ohne euch ist gar kein Problem. Da wird Sicherheit ganz großgeschrieben. Ich werde entweder zum Flughafen oder Bahnhof gebracht und es wird sichergestellt, dass ich in meinen Zug oder zu meinem Flugsteig komme.
(Seid ihr jetzt beruhigt?)

Topic 29: Immigration to the US

91 a)

Tom wants to know …	*Tom will wissen …*
… how emigrants from Bavaria got to the US.	***… wie Auswanderer aus Bayern in die Vereinigten Staaten kamen.***
… what made life on the ships so hard.	***… was die Überfahrt erschwerte. / … was den Aufenthalt auf den Schiffen so beschwerlich machte.***
… how the journey by ship changed in the 19th century?	***… wie sich Schiffsreisen im 19. Jahrhundert veränderten. / … was sich im 19. Jahrhundert an Schiffsreisen änderte.***

b) *Zur ersten Frage vgl. Absatz eins und zwei. Die Informationen zur zweiten Frage finden sich in Absatz vier. Die letzte Frage kann man anhand des letzten Absatzes beantworten.*

c)

der Ausbau des Eisenbahnnetzes	railway connections were improved/became better/ there were more and more trains
Flussschiff	**a ship (travelling) on rivers**
Überseehafen	**ports from which ships go overseas/go to America (and Australia)**
Verpflegung	**something to eat/food**
das rasch wachsende Angebot an Überfahrtsplätzen	**the number of places on ships to America rose/ increased quickly/the quick increase in places on ships to America/there were suddenly more and more places on ships to America**

d) *(Lösungsvorschlag)*

Hi Tom

Good to hear from you. I hope you enjoyed your vacation.
It's funny, we're talking about immigration to the US in our English class, too. So let's see if I can help you.
In the first half of the 19th century, emigrants from Bavaria had to travel to Le Havre (France), Rotterdam (the Netherlands) or Liverpool (England). They walked part of the way, went by cart or horse-drawn coach and finally took ships along the big German rivers (Rhine, Main, Weser) to get to the coast. From 1850 on, they could use trains to get to Bremerhaven and Hamburg, the German ports where ships left for the US.
There were too many passengers on the ships and they didn't have enough fresh air. Also sanitary conditions were bad and they didn't have enough food. So many passengers died.
In the 19th century more and more steamers were built and used for the journey. They were much quicker and traveled to the US in about 15 days, whereas sailing ships took about 12 weeks. However, the journey on a steamer was very expensive in the beginning. So most people still had to use sailing ships because the journey was cheaper. However, in 1870 about 88 % of all ships were steamers. So there were more places for passengers and therefore the tickets became cheaper and the journey less difficult.

Hope that helps!

Yours

Finn

Topic 30: Strategien zur Sprachmittlung

92 *(Lösungsvorschlag)*

Mediation Strategies

Vor der Sprachmittlung:

- ➥ Wer ist der Adressat? Wie wird dieser angesprochen? (S. 84)
- ➥ Mit welcher Absicht wird gemittelt? (S. 84)
- ➥ Welche Inhalte sind wichtig für die Sprachmittlung? (S. 84)
- ➥ Bei geschriebenen Texten die entsprechenden Stellen markieren (S. 92)
- ➥ Bei Hörtexten entsprechende Notizen anfertigen
- ➥ Welcher Zieltext soll erstellt werden (z. B. E-Mail, Vortrag) und was sind typische Merkmale dieser Textsorte?

Während der Sprachmittlung:

- ➥ Was muss ggf. ergänzt werden?
  - zusätzliche Informationen bei sehr kurzen Texten (S. 84)
  - landestypische Begriffe (S. 88)
  - Höflichkeitsfloskeln
- ➥ Was muss ggf. weggelassen werden? (S. 90)
- ➥ Wörter im Wörterbuch nachschlagen (S. 92, 96)
- ➥ Den Stil des Zieltextes beachten (S. 103)
- ➥ unbekannte Wörter umschreiben (S. 102)

Nach der Sprachmittlung:

- ➥ Schriftliche Zieltexte nochmals in Hinblick auf die Überlegungen, die du im Vorfeld angestellt hast, überprüfen (S. 103)
- ➥ Sprache überprüfen (S. 103)

Writing

Topic 31: A day in NYC

93 a) Your email should be …

- [ ] very short.
- [x] nice and friendly.
- [x] polite.
- [ ] funny.

b) What should you write about?

- [x] You should give information about your trip and your experiences.
- [ ] You have to give them historical information about New York.
- [x] Your description should be positive rather than negative because you do not want your host parents to worry about you.
- [ ] You can complain about everything that you did not like there.

c) What language should you use?

- [ ] You write in German.
- [ ] You write in formal English.
- [x] You write in informal English.

94 *(Lösungsvorschlag)*

- Where: New York
- Why: Sightseeing
- Who: **other exchange students**

Sightseeing trip that day		
When	**Where/What**	**What it was like**
8 a.m.	arrival by bus at ferry terminal in Manhattan; you could see the Statue of Liberty	awesome and breathtaking to see the Statue of Liberty
after arrival	Statue of Liberty, climbed steps up to the crown	quite narrow staircase, fantastic view of Ellis Island

half an hour later	Ellis Island, museum; photos showing immigrants	not boring, actually pretty cool
after we returned to the bus	bus tour; 9/11 Memorial	glad to be able to sit, moved by the many names on the bronze panels
lunchtime	Chinatown, lunch at a restaurant	delicious; shops and restaurants all truly Chinese
afternoon	Empire State Building	waiting took forever, view was breathtaking at sunset
dinnertime	hot dog stand	yummy
evening	arrival at the youth hostel	pretty rundown, but clean

95 Dear Cathy

L.A. is just absolutely awesome! Chloe and I had such a fantastic day today! After a long night on the bus, we arrived in Hollywood early in the morning. The first thing we went to was the Walk of Fame! That was truly amazing! It suddenly hit home that we really are in Los Angeles!

Totally thrilled, we booked a Movie Stars' Homes Tour on a minibus. Now, you probably think, "Oh no, seeing the homes of celebrities hidden behind huge fences, that must be boring!", but our tour guide was actually great fun and gave us lots of information on how the rich and the famous live. We also drove past some important sights, such as the Hollywood Sign. It was quite an experience being there!

After a few hours the bus took us to a restaurant which sold chicken and waffles. The food was delicious. After that, we walked through the streets and did some shopping.

In the afternoon we took a bus to Santa Monica Pier, which took forever, but it paid off, as the sun was setting when we reached the beach!

On our way to the hostel we stopped at an Italian deli and bakery and had a yummy sandwich for dinner.

When we finally made it home to our youth hostel, I was so excited that I didn't care that the youth hostel was quite rundown. Chloe was a little shocked. My room, however, is clean, so don't worry!

See you soon,

Koray

96 *(Lösungsvorschlag)*

Dear Linda and Brian

New York is just absolutely awesome!

The other exchange students and I had such a fantastic day today! After a long night on the bus, we arrived at the ferry terminal in Manhattan at about 8 a.m., and the first thing we saw was the Statue of Liberty! That was truly amazing! It suddenly hit home that we really are in New York!

Totally thrilled, we took the ferry to Staten Island and climbed the narrow steps up the statue to the crown. The view was just fantastic, as you could see Ellis Island, our next stop.

Half an hour later, the ferry took us to Ellis Island. I thought, "Oh no, a museum – that will be boring!", but the former immigration station is actually pretty cool. There are lots of old photos showing immigrants. It was quite an experience being there!

We returned to our bus and we were glad to be able to just sit and drive past some important sights in Manhattan. We only got off the bus briefly to have a look at the 9/11 Memorial.

The bus took us to a famous Chinese restaurant, where we had lunch. The food was delicious. After that, we walked through the streets of Chinatown, and we really felt like we were in China.

In the afternoon, we went to the Empire State Building, as we wanted to enjoy the marvellous view. The queuing took forever, but the long wait paid off, as the sun was setting when we reached the top!

On our way to the hostel we stopped at a small hot dog booth, where we all had a hot dog for dinner.

When we finally made it home to our youth hostel, we were all so excited about our first day in New York that we didn't care that the youth hostel was quite rundown. My room, however, is clean, so don't worry!

Take care,
Mia

97 *(Lösungsvorschlag)*

Chloe Hamilton
7740 West Academy Avenue
Lakewood, CO 80226

LA Youth Hostel
1212 Ocean Blvd
Los Angeles, CA 90028

May 28, 2018

Re: Complaint about dirty room

Dear Sir or Madam

I am writing to complain about a dirty room at your hostel.

On May 18, 2018, I stayed at the LA Youth Hostel for one night in room number 201. As I already told the person at the reception at the time, this room had not been cleaned properly after previous guests had checked out. There was trash on the floor, the bedlinen had stains and there was hair all over the bathroom.

When I asked to be moved to another room, I was told that this was not possible, as the hostel was booked up. The receptionist promised to have my room cleaned immediately. Unfortunately, that never happened. In the end, I fell asleep on the chair and left your hostel without having a shower.

I would therefore like you to refund the $ 64 I paid for the room.

I look forward to hearing from you very soon.

Sincerely
Chloe Hamilton

98 *(Lösungsvorschlag)*

Subject: Back home safely

Dear all

How are you? Did you get home from the airport all right? Thanks again for taking me there with all my luggage!

You'll be glad to hear that I had a safe journey home! Everything went well. My parents picked me up at Frankfurt Airport, which was very nice. It's really good to see them again and to be back home.

But I already miss you and my life in the US, too. I had a fantastic year because I went to a great school, made really good friends and – above all – had the best host family ever! Thank you so much for letting me be part of your family, for helping me whenever I had problems and for always making me feel at home!

Hope to hear from you soon!

Lots of love
Tim

Topic 32: Celebrating Thanksgiving in the US

99 b) *(Lösungsvorschlag)*

Thanksgiving

Who was there:
host family and I, Grandpa Jim, Grandma Katherine, Uncle Robert, his wife Anne and their sons

Where:
house of grandparents of host family (= farm)

What you did and how it was:

– *arrival at farm after long drive*	*warm welcome*
– *helping in the kitchen*	*fantastic smells, laughter*
– *watching American football game on TV*	*great fun, shouting*
– *prayer*	*strange*
– *traditional Thanksgiving meal*	*really good*
– *clearing up the table, watching a parade on TV*	
– *playing American football in the garden*	*hard work after eating so much*

What food:
- *roast turkey*
- *sweet corn that looked like a bowl of jewels*
- *gravy*
- *peas from the garden*
- *pumpkin pie*

→ *smelled delicious*
→ *tasted really good*

What you liked best and why:
American football → great fun watching and playing it

100 *(Lösungsvorschlag)*

Sense	
seeing	• that looked like a bowl of jewels (the sweet corn)
tasting	• really good (Thanksgiving meal)
feeling	• strange (prayer) • welcome (arrival at farm)
smelling	• delicious (Thanksgiving meal)
hearing	• laughter (while cooking) • shouting (during football)

101 *(Lösungsvorschlag)*

23 November 20…

Dear Diary

Thanksgiving is a holiday that only exists in the USA, so I was very curious about it. Looking back at yesterday's events, I have to say it's been the best day of my year as an exchange student so far.

My host family and I were invited to the farm of Grandma Katherine and Grandpa Jim. We got up early and drove for hours. When we arrived, Uncle Robert, Aunt Anne and their sons were already there. After a warm welcome, everybody had to help in the kitchen. We were all really happy and the room was full of laughter. The food already smelled delicious.

Uncle Robert and Grandpa Jim were the first to finish their jobs, so, they started to watch American football on TV. One by one we joined them and there was a lot of cheering and shouting. It was great fun and it felt a bit like the World Cup at home. Luckily, the family's favourite team won the match and only shortly afterwards the meal was ready.

We all sat down at the table and there was a huge roast turkey. Around it there were mashed potatoes, dark brown gravy, yellow sweet corn that looked like a bowl of jewels, big peas from Grandma Katherine's garden and pumpkin pie. After saying, "Oh, wow!", everybody was silent and Grandpa Jim started a Thanksgiving prayer, thanking God for the family's well-being. Not used to prayers, I felt strange, but I joined in saying "Amen". Then the food was passed around. It tasted so good!

After that Uncle Robert and Aunt Anne cleared the table and then started watching a Thanksgiving parade on TV. My host parents and all of us teenagers went outside and started playing American football. It was hard work for me after so much food!

All in all, I can say that I experienced a traditional Thanksgiving party and enjoyed it a lot, especially the food. But the best thing about this American holiday was watching American football on TV with my host family and later playing it myself. I'll have to teach my brothers at home!

102 *(Lösungsvorschlag)*

25 December 20...

Dear Diary
Christmas is so different in the USA! Celebrating it with my host family rather than my own family was strange. However, I really had a great time and did not get homesick!

The biggest difference, of course, is not getting the presents on Christmas Eve. Yesterday morning, I was really afraid that I would start missing home and our family Christmas while sitting alone under a Christmas tree with lots of colorful lights and too many decorations. But that never happened because my host family is just great and organized a big Christmas Eve party with all my new friends. We had my favorite American snacks and lots of fun until very late at night. So I fell asleep happily.

This morning, I woke up totally excited about my Christmas presents. Running down the stairs, I heard that my host family was already in the living-room, wishing each other "Merry Christmas". When I joined them, I was hugged by everyone and that was when I truly felt at home! Then all of us looked into our stockings hanging over the fireplace and we had a great time opening presents and eating delicious food. We never made it out of our pajama pants today – that was just great! I was so happy today that I almost forgot to phone my parents!

Anyway, my American Christmas experience will continue tomorrow, so I'd better get some sleep now!

Topic 33: To catch a thief

103 a) Look at the following aspects and decide what belongs in the first sentence of your summary.

- [x] author
- [x] title
- [ ] length of the text
- [x] form of text, e. g. newspaper article, (short) story, poem
- [x] date/year of publication
- [ ] place of publication
- [x] short description of what the text is about (who? what? where? when?)
- [ ] personal opinion on the text

b) In a summary, which of the following are do's and which are don'ts?

	do	don't
❶ use your own words	✓	
❷ use quotes from the text/direct speech		✓
❸ use mostly present tenses	✓	
❹ use the first person (e. g. "I think", "In my opinion")		✓
❺ use short forms (e. g. "hasn't", "won't")		✓
❻ include details on the persons in the text		✓

104
- Who: **a teenage boy**
- What: **tries to steal a pair of jeans**
- Where: **in a store (clothing store or department store)**
- When: **at about 3:30 pm ("But 6 o'clock was still more than two hours away" ll. 18/19)**

105 *(Lösungsvorschlag)*

Passages	Keywords/-phrases	Headline
ll. 1–4	"screwdriver" (l. 1) "razor blade" (l. 1) "cut myself" (l. 2) "stain the 501 jeans" (l. 3) "everybody could tell" (l. 4)	Afraid of removing the tag with a razor blade
ll. 5–13	"had not been too easy to get hold of a razor blade" (l. 5) "father and his older brother Dwane preferred electric razors" (ll. 5/6) "going through her arts utensils he had found the blade" (ll. 11/12)	How the boy got the razor blade
ll. 14–19	"busy" (l. 14) "Parents were trying to do their shopping and keep an eye on their kids" (ll. 14/15) "Shop assistants hated this time" (ll. 16/17) "looked tired" (l. 17) "6 o'clock was still more than two hours away" (ll. 18/19) "enough time" (l. 19)	Perfect timing for shoplifting
ll. 20–37	"most expensive jeans in his size" (ll. 21/22) "three items at a time into the changing room" (ll. 22/23) "convenient" (l. 23) "carefully" (l. 24) "remove the tag" (ll. 24/25) "tag came off" (l. 26) "Wearing two pairs of jeans" (ll. 27/28) "knew he would be alright" (ll. 28/29) "make it home" (l. 29) "passed the electronic theft-protection gate without any trouble" (ll. 36/37) "smiled to himself" (l. 37)	Theft of an expensive pair of jeans/Everything goes according to plan

ll. 37–40	"store detective" (l. 39) "follow me to my office" (ll. 39/40)	Stopped by the store detective

106 a) The short story "**To Catch a Thief**" written **by** Rainer Jacob and **published** in 1997 is **about** a **teenager/teenage boy/young man** who **tries to** steal a pair of jeans from a **store/shop/department store**.

b) *(Lösungsvorschlag)*

- A teenage boy carries a screwdriver and a razor.
- He is worried that he will hurt himself when using the razor.
- ~~finding a screwdriver at home = easy~~
- ~~finding a razor = very hard~~
- ~~His older brother Dwane and his father like electric razors.~~
- ~~He has been afraid to ask his mum whether she has any razors because she might ask questions.~~
- ~~He has taken the razor from his sister's arts class material.~~
- The young man is happy that he picked the right time for shoplifting: ~~about 3:30 pm.~~
- The shop assistants won't pay much attention to him.
- They are weary: they have already been working for hours.
- They have a lot to do because the shop is full of families.
- lots of time to get everything done
- Everything goes according to plan.
- He picks the jeans that cost the most ~~and two more pairs of jeans to throw on the rack later on.~~
- ~~goes to a cubicle~~
- Inside the changing room, he uses the screwdriver and the razor to get the tag off. ~~"Don't cut into the fine cloth," he told himself.~~
- Wearing the stolen jeans under his old jeans he goes down towards the exit and passes the electronic theft-protection gate successfully.
- At that moment, ~~right before leaving the shop,~~ the store detective stops the thief and takes the young man to his office.

107 *(Lösungsvorschlag)*

The short story "To Catch a Thief" written by Rainer Jacob and published in 1997 is about a teenage boy's attempt to steal a pair of jeans from a store.

At the beginning of the story, the young man hopes that the theft will go well and that he will not hurt himself while working on the tag on the jeans with a razor. Inside the shop, he is happy to notice that he has picked the right time for his task because the place is full of people, the shop assistants are tired and he has got more than enough time before the store closes. In the men's department, the young thief starts by picking the jeans that cost the most. Then he goes into a changing room and uses the screwdriver and the razor to get the tag off. Wearing the stolen jeans under his old jeans the teenage boy walks down towards the exit confidently and passes the electronic theft-protection gate successfully. It is at that moment that the store detective stops him and takes the young man to his office.

Topic 34: Tornado in Iowa

108 *(Lösungsvorschlag)*

- There is a completely destroyed wooden house in the middle.
- Parts of the walls, windows and lots of pieces of furniture are lying on the grass outside what is left of the house.
- There are tree branches and pieces of a big tree trunk everywhere.
- Another house is damaged (destroyed roof and upper floor).
- You can see a damaged car.
- Two houses in the background seem to be in good condition – they were maybe not hit by the tornado at all.
- There are many dark clouds still in the sky above the scene.
- People are trying to clean up the mess.
- Maybe some people are looking for personal belongings.

109

PLOT

What happens first, next, after that?

- tornado warning on the radio while Susan and Greg were renovating Susan's new house
- first they stayed calm – they knew what to do and they thought, the tornado would not hit them anyway
- then they went outside and saw the dark cloud and decided to seek shelter; but there was no storm cellar
- moments later they saw the tornado and felt the wind
- they ran into the house, taking shelter in a closet under the stair-case
- tornado hit the house
- the roof and the first floor were ripped off
- after seven minutes the tornado was gone, Susan and Greg both fine
- Greg and Susan now realised they loved each other and kissed for the first time

MAIN CHARACTER

Female Susan

Age 30

What is she like?

nice, friendly, likes to laugh

What relationship do they have?

- old friends and former schoolmates
- Greg is secretly in love with Susan
- Susan likes him a lot

MAIN CHARACTER

Male Greg

Age 30

What is he like?

nice, friendly, quieter than Susan, enjoys helping Susan

110

Exposition	3
Rising action	1
Climax	4
Falling action	2

111 *(Lösungsvorschlag)*

	Plot	Atmosphere	
		adjectives/ adverbs	description of details
Exposition	• tornado warning on the radio / Susan and Greg were renovating Susan's new house	• sunny	• Susan and Greg were just taking a break.
Rising action	• They stayed calm/ remembered what to do during a tornado. • Greg thought that the tornado wouldn't hit them. • saw the dark cloud/ decided to seek shelter; no storm cellar • saw the tornado and felt the wind • ran back to the house, taking shelter in a closet • Greg tried to comfort Susan.	• large, dark (cloud) • silent • uneasy • nervously • a bit panicky • like a huge, black skyscraper • terribly fast • strong wind	• looked at each other and smiled reassuringly • wind blew strongly through Susan's hair • Greg's face went white. • He grabbed her hand.
Climax	• tornado hit the house • roof and the first floor were ripped off	• like a train or more like an airplane	• Greg threw himself across Susan to protect her. • Their mouths filled with dirt.
Falling action	• Susan and Greg relieved that they both seem to be fine • Susan knew they would face whatever was out there together.	• slowly • fine • not hurt	• felt they had been in the eye of the storm for hours, not just minutes • Susan fell into Greg's arms. • He kissed her head. • She started to cry.

112 *Beide Varianten möglich.*

113 (*Lösungsvorschlag*)

Lost and Found

Susan had bought this small house in Woodward only a week before. Her parents and friends had helped her renovate her first house. It was Greg, an old schoolfriend, who was still helping that sunny Saturday afternoon. They were enjoying a short coffee break, when they heard the tornado warning on the radio.

For a moment, they were silent. They looked at each other and smiled reassuringly while remembering their school training about what to do when you get a tornado warning. Greg thought that like so many other tornados in the past, this tornado would not hit Woodward. Still, they went outside and saw a large, dark cloud. The wind was blowing strongly through Susan's hair. "We'd better seek shelter," Susan said nervously. "You do have a storm cellar under the house or in the garden, right?" Greg was starting to feel uneasy as well. "Susan?" "Ah, no. I didn't think of it when I bought the house." Susan answered, feeling a bit panicky. "Now stay calm, Susan! What's the safest place in the house?" Suddenly Greg's face went white. There it was, the tornado, like a huge, black skyscraper, moving towards them terribly fast. "Go!" Greg screamed, feeling over the wind, grabbing her hand. They closed the front door to keep the very strong wind out. Susan saw the closet under the old staircase. "Let's get in there, Greg, that's our best chance!" Susan knelt down, covering her head with her arms. Greg quickly got in as well, saying, "We'll be fine, Susan, we'll be fine!"

Only seconds later, the noise came, like a train or more like an airplane, Susan thought. That was when they knew that the tornado was directly over their heads. Without thinking, Greg threw himself across Susan to protect her. Suddenly their mouths filled with dirt and they realized that the roof and the first floor must have been taken off. "Please, go away, please go away!" Susan said to herself.

By the time it finally did, Susan felt they had been in the eye of the storm for hours, not just seven minutes. "Greg? Are you okay?" He was getting up slowly. "I think I'm fine. And you?" "I'm fine. Greg, … thank you!" Susan fell into his arms and felt his lips kissing her head. That was the moment she started to cry. They were not hurt and they would face what was waiting for them outside the closet together.

114 *Individuelle Lösungen*

Topic 35: "Cliques are good for teenagers!"

115 *(Lösungsvorschlag)*

I would like to belong to clique **B** because **the teenagers in the picture seem to be friendly and enjoying their time together.**

Clique **A** is a group I would not want to belong to because **the teenagers in the picture seem to be unfriendly, aggressive and maybe even drunk.**

116 *(Lösungsvorschlag)*

Statement: **"Cliques are good/dangerous for teenagers"**	
+ **(advantages)**	**–** **(disadvantages)**
• cliques give teenagers a feeling of belonging ➡ self-confidence grows • teenagers in a clique always find someone who has time for them and shares the same interests, opinions and style ➡ never bored, but have lots of fun • teenagers always have people they can share their happiness and their problems with ➡ support, security • in a clique, teenagers have to agree on many things (like their plans for the weekend, etc.) ➡ a clique helps them to learn how to compromise	• cliques share certain interests and exclude others who are different ➡ outsiders • peer pressure ➡ no individuality, you have to be like the others, you may have to do things you do not really want to do • cliques often have a leader: leader can be mean and tell others what to do ➡ members of a clique might feel they have nothing to say
Your opinion: **Cliques can be dangerous, but in general being part of a clique has a lot of benefits for a teenager if the people in the clique are okay.**	

117

topic sentence	Cliques are groups of people that share interests and exclude people who are different.
explanation (supporting sentences)	In every school there are different cliques because there is a great number of different things that people can have in common. Teenagers who are not part of these groups are left out.
example(s) (supporting sentences)	For example, loving the same kind of music, being a fan of the same sport, etc. can be the reason why teenagers are in a clique together.

118

Topic sentence 1	**A clique weakens a teenager's self-confidence.**	☐
Topic sentence 2	**A clique makes a teenager more confident.**	☑
Topic sentence 3	**There are reasons why teenagers often feel insecure.**	☐
Topic sentence 4	**Teenagers join a clique to no longer feel alone.**	☐

119 a)

supporting sentences	**If other teenagers are mean to you, the people in your clique will help you. They will study with you whenever you get bad grades at school. They will give you advice when you have problems with other teenagers, teachers or your parents. They will listen and be happy for you when something wonderful happens. It can be great to be part of a supportive clique.**

b) <u>For example</u>, if other teenagers are mean to you, the people from your clique will help you. <u>Furthermore</u>, they will study with you whenever you get bad grades at school. <u>Even more importantly</u>, they will give you advice when you have problems with other teenagers, teachers or your parents. <u>At the same time</u>, they will listen and be happy for you when something wonderful happens. <u>As a result</u>, it can be great to be part of a supportive clique.

120/21 *(Lösungsvorschlag)*

Cliques are good for teenagers

During their time at school most teenagers are part of a certain group. Although a clique has more benefits than dangers, it depends on the people in the clique whether it is actually good or dangerous for teenagers.

One important danger lies in the fact that cliques are groups of people that share interests and exclude people who are different. In every school there are different cliques because there are a great number of different things people can have in common. Loving the same kind of music or being a fan of the same sport, for example, can be the reason why teenagers are together in a clique. Teenagers who are not part of these groups are left out.

Another great danger is bad leaders. If cliques have leaders who use their influence and power to tell the other people in their group what to do, it can happen that these teenagers start to obey them without questioning, because they are afraid. It is the fear of having to leave the clique and thus lose their friends that makes them follow orders. As a result, they might do bad things they normally would not do.

On the other hand, a clique has very important benefits. One of them is making young people more self-confident. Teenagers are on their way from childhood to becoming adults, so they have to cope with physical and emotional changes. Because of that some young people feel insecure. Mostly they have the impression that adults like their parents do not understand them, so they often join a clique to have a place where they fit in and belong. Here they have other teenagers that have the same interests. As a result, they feel understood, accepted and secure and thus their self-confidence increases.

Most importantly, a clique provides support through the ups and downs of teenage life. Members of a clique always have people that are there for them. For example, if a teenager is attacked by others, the people in the clique will help him/her. Furthermore, they will reassure him/her whenever he/she gets bad exam results and give advice when he/she has problems with other teenagers, teachers or parents. Equally importantly, they will listen and be happy for him/her when something wonderful happens. As a result, the support of a good clique is its greatest benefit.

As a conclusion, one can say that cliques generally hold more benefits for teenagers than dangers. However, it is the people in the clique that make it either good or dangerous.

122 *Mögliche Argumente:*

Arguments against the thesis:

- Animals in zoos live in safety and security.
- They get a lot of care that they do not get in the wild (e.g. food, medical treatment).
- Zoos make it possible for children and adults to observe (wild) animals up close. ➡ Education
- Animals in captivity allow researchers *(Forscher)* and scientists *(Wissenschaftler)* to do their studies easily.
  ➡ What they find out might help the animals in the wild.
- Zoos help wild animals that are on the list of endangered species to survive.
  ➡ Some animals are still hunted for their skins or bones.
  ➡ Some have little chance to survive because of pollution, the destruction of their habitat, diseases etc.
- Zoos have breeding programs *(Zuchtprogramme)*.
  ➡ That way it is made sure that endangered animals do not die out.

Arguments for the thesis:

- Animals in zoos are forced to live in small spaces.
  ➡ Especially wild animals that hunt (e.g. lions) or walk long distances (e.g. elephants) have problems living in small places.
  ➡ Lions can become quite aggressive.
  ➡ Dangerous for the zookeepers
- Animals are captured and held in captivity for human entertainment.
- The natural behavior of the animals changes in captivity *(Gefangenschaft)*.
- It takes a long time for animals captured from the wild to get used to living in captivity and this puts them under stress.
- Animals born in zoos cannot be set free, as they do not know how to hunt for themselves.
  ➡ The breeding programs do nothing for the numbers of endangered animals in the wild.

123 *Mögliche Argumente:*

Arguments for the thesis:

- Students often do not pay attention to the traffic while walking to school because they are only concentrating on their mobiles.
  ➡ Lots of accidents happen.
- Students might use their phones secretly in class to chat, etc.

➡ They do not pay attention to the lessons.

- If students constantly use their phone, even during breaks, they do not learn how to communicate with people face to face (no social skills).
- Students might use the phone to pass around false or negative information about others quickly. ➡ Bullying that cannot easily be remedied.
- Photos and videos can be taken of other students and teachers secretly.
  ➡ That material might be used to hurt people.
- Phones can get lost, broken or stolen.
- Phones can be used to cheat in exams.

Arguments against the thesis:

- Mobile phones are necessary for safety, especially on the way to school and back home.
  ➡ If anything happens, they can always phone their parents/school.
- Teachers can make sure that the mobile phones are switched off during the lessons.
- Parents, children and friends can contact each other quickly if they need to change plans or ask questions.
- Bullying also happens without mobile phones.
- Mobile phones can be very useful in lessons, for example, when it is necessary to do some quick internet research.

Topic 36: Strategien zum Schreiben

124 *(Lösungsvorschlag)*

Writing Strategies
Vor dem Schreiben: ➡ sich in die Situation versetzen (S. 106) ➡ überlegen, wer der Adressat ist (S. 106) ➡ Sprachstil auswählen (persönlich/formell) (S. 106) ➡ Ideen sammeln, z. B. in Tabelle, Mindmap, mit W-Fragen (S. 107) ➡ Für Zusammenfassung: Text in Sinnabschnitte gliedern, Teilüberschriften erstellen
Während des Schreibens: ➡ für Beschreibungen ausdrucksstarke Adjektive, Adverbien und beschreibende Relativsätze verwenden (S. 108, 129) ➡ das Geschriebene muss zur Rolle passen (z. B. Tagebucheintrag) (S. 115) ➡ richtigen Aufbau der Textform beachten: Brief ➡ S. 110–113, Tagebucheintrag ➡ S. 115/116, Zusammenfassung ➡ S. 122, 124, Geschichte ➡ S. 127–130, Kommentar ➡ S. 132/133, 135/136; meist Einleitung, Hauptteil, Schluss ➡ textspezifische Redemittel verwenden, z. B. Sinneswahrnehmungen bei Erlebnissen (S. 116)
Nach dem Schreiben: ➡ Sprachrichtigkeit kontrollieren (z. B. Zeiten, Rechtschreibung, false friends, he/she/it „s" im simple present) ➡ Sprachstil prüfen (förmlich /persönlich) (S. 111) ➡ Textgliederung prüfen (Absätze) (S. 111) ➡ „connectives" einbauen (S. 111)

Bildnachweis

Cover: © Nikada/istockphoto

Reading

S.1 rez_art. 123rf.com; S. 5 Foto: TydeNet/wikipedia, CC BY-SA 3.0; S. 6 Foto (Warning): Wyp/wikipedia, CC BY-SA 3.0; S. 7 Foto (the Min Min Light): www.gondwananet.com/ wikipedia, CC BY-SA 3.0; S. 8 Foto (Truancy Hotline): Kyriaki from Deerfield Beach, US of A/wikipedia, CC BY-SA 3.0, Foto (Golf): Redaktion; S. 9 © Elnur/Dreamstime.com; S. 10 leaves: jordygraph. 123rf.com, group of students: highwaystarz. 123rf.com, notebook: iunewind. 123rf.com, globe: argus. Shutterstock; S. 13 Sam Chadwick. Shutterstock; S. 16 wooden house: kzww. Shutterstock, calendar: Stephen Rees. Shutterstock, playing football: Iakov Filimonov. Shutterstock, golf: Sashkin. Shutterstock; S. 17 canoe: auremar. 123rf.com, tree: bestofgreenscreen. Shutterstock, climbing equipment: Vixit. Shutterstock, goodbye: Rawpixel.com. Shutterstock; S. 18 Arcady. Shutterstock; S. 21 ©leekrob - Can Stock Photo Inc.; S 24 Konstantin Chagin. Shutterstock; S. 28 Uluc Ceylani. Shutterstock; S. 31 Hasloo Group Production Studio. Shutterstock; S. 32 Helen Strong. Shutterstock; S. 33 kuleczka. Shutterstock

Listening

S. 35 Piotr Wawrzyniuk. Shutterstock; S. 37 123rf.com; S: 40 owling: jrsnchzhrs/flickr, CC BY-ND 2.0, Vadering: David Geitgey Sierralupe/flickr, CC BY 2.0, catbreading: steve lyon/flickr, CC BY-SA 2.0, planking: Matteo Paciotti/flickr, CC BY 2.0; S. 42 Monkey Business Images. Shutterstock; S. 44 teepees: David P. Lewis. Shutterstock, Inukshuk: Stephen B. Goodwin. Shutterstock; S. 45 Ariwasabi. Shutterstock; S. 47 Sabphoto. Shutterstock; S. 49 hotel: Christian Mueller. Shutterstock, Nuraghe: cameris. 123rf.com, Su Portu beach: gevision. 123rf.com; S. 50 Petrafler. Shutterstock; S. 52 © RyersonClark/istockphoto

Words

S: 57 jcjgphotography. Shutterstock; S. 58 tammykayphoto. 123rf.com; S. 59 123rf.com; S. 60 william87. 123rf.com; S. 68 James Steidl. Shutterstock; S. 69 surprised: © Emil Durov/ Dreamstime.com, shocked: © Olga Sapegina/Dreamstime.com, enthusiastic: ©Wavebreakmedia LTD/Dreamstime.com, unhappy: ©Ruslan Kokarev/Dreamstime.com, annoyed: ©Jabiru/ Dreamstime.com; S. 76 Mayflower: aceshot1. Shutterstock, Plymoth Plantation: David Persson. Shutterstock; S. 77 Christophe Testi. Shutterstock; S. 78/79 bulletin board: Monkey Business Images. Shutterstock, wastepaper basket: Gergo Orban. Shutterstock, boys with smartphones: Monkey Business Images. Shutterstock, thumbs up: Andy Dean Photography. Shutterstock, subway: Elenamiv. Shutterstock, motorcycle: © Sutichak/Dreamstime.com, French fries: Rikaphoto. Shutterstock, potato chips: © Can Stock Photo/leeser; S. 80 laboratory/vet: 123rf.com, hot coffee: CREATISTA. Shutterstock, party: oliveromg. Shutterstock, internet: imtmphoto. Shutterstock

Mediation

S. 83 © Rawpixelimages/Dreamstime.com; S. 84 © Kawee Wateesatogkij/Dreamstime.com; S. 85 shopping mall: © Athenar/Dreamstime.com, banner: © Ekostsov/Dreamstime.com; S. 86 supermarket: © Vtt Studio/Dreamstime.com, menu: © Vtt Studio/Dreamstime.com; S. 87 racorn. Shutterstock; S. 89 Matthias Stolt/adobe stock; S. 91, 99 designmaestro. Shutterstock; S. 92 keithlevit. 123rf.com; S. 93 alert: Oleksiy Mark. Shutterstock, phone: zentilia. Shutterstock, fire extinguisher: udaix. Shutterstock, hands: ullrich. Shutterstock, stairs: Arcady. Shutterstock, assembly point: © Adonis1969/Dreamstime.com; S. 95 Monkey Business Images. Shutterstock; S. 97, 98 iunewind. 123rf.com

Writing

S. 105 stockbroker. 123rf.com; S. 106. 1038688. Shutterstock; S. 107 bus: © Giovanni Gagliardi/Dreamstime.com, Ellis Island: gary718. Shutterstock, Chinatown: © Kmiragaya/Dreamstime.com, Statue of Liberty: Vlad G. Shutterstock, 9/11 Memorial: © Almaz888/Dreamstime.com, group of teenage friends: William Perugini. Shutterstock; S. 109 designmaestro. Shutterstock; S. 110 boy: GaudiLab. Shutterstock, girl: 123rf.com, envelope: Angela Waye. Shutterstock; S. 113 ifong. 123rf.com; S. 114 family: © Monkey Business Images – Dreamstime.com, notebook: iunewind. 123rf.com; S. 115 person and house: vector illustration. Shutterstock, figure with question mark: Leremy. Shutterstock, chicken: Freud. Shutterstock; S. 117 iunewind. 123rf.com; S. 119 glamour. Shutterstock; S. 123 Galyna Andrushko. Shutterstock; S. 125 iunewind. 123rf.com; S. 126 US National Weather Service; S. 128 starsstudio. 123rf.com; S. 131 drinking teenagers: Monkey Business Images. Shutterstock, cheerfull teenagers: Iakov Filimonov. Shutterstock; S. 137 monkey: tomgigabite. Shutterstock, writing: Syda Productions. Shutterstock

Lösungen

S. 147 Sashkin. Shutterstock; S. 154 Arcady. Shutterstock; S. 166 123rf.com; S. 179 Petrafler. Shutterstock; S. 190/191 surprised: © Emil Durov/Dreamstime.com, shocked: © Olga Sapegina/Dreamstime.com, enthusiastic: ©Wavebreakmedia LTD/Dreamstime.com, unhappy: ©Ruslan Kokarev/Dreamstime.com, annoyed: ©Jabiru/Dreamstime.com; S. 196 laboratory/vet: 123rf.com, hot coffee: CREATISTA. Shutterstock, party: oliveromg. Shutterstock, internet: imtmphoto. Shutterstock; S. 202 alert: Oleksiy Mark. Shutterstock, phone: zentilia. Shutterstock, fire extinguisher: udaix. Shutterstock, hands: ullrich. Shutterstock, stairs: Arcady. Shutterstock, assembly point: © Adonis1969/Dreamstime.com; S. 207 iunewind. 123rf.com